The Definitive
CANADIAN
WINE &
CHEESE
COOKBOOK

The Definitive CANADIAN WINE & CHEESE COOKBOOK

Gurth Pretty & Tony Aspler

whitecap

EDITING	ELAINE JONES
PROOFREADING	JOAN E. TEMPLETON
INTERIOR DESIGN & ILLUSTRATION	GRACE PARTRIDGE
ADDITIONAL TYPESETTING	CHRISSY DAVEY
FOOD PHOTOGRAPHY	GEOFFREY ROSS
FOOD STYLING	RYAN JENNINGS
COVER DESIGN & PHOTOGRAPH	MICHELLE MAYNE

Printed in Canada

LIBRARY AND ARCHIVES CANADA CATALOGUING IN PUBLICATION

Pretty, Gurth
The definitive Canadian wine and cheese cookbook / Gurth Pretty, Tony Aspler.

Includes index.
ISBN 978-1-55285-896-7
ISBN 1-55285-896-0

1. Cookery (Wine). 2. Cookery (Cheese). 3. Cheese. 4. Wine and wine making.
5. Cookery, Canadian. I. Aspler, Tony, 1939- II. Title.

TX726.P74 2007   641.2'2C2   007-901705-3

*The publisher acknowledges the financial support of the Government of Canada through the Book
Publishing Industry Development Program (BPIDP) and the province of British Columbia through the
Book Publishing Tax Credit.*

For Joanne Thank you for all the hats you wear; you are my muse, grocery shopper, and my head recipe taster. You were in the kitchen with me, helping to prepare the ingredients and providing me with your suggestions for improvements. Together, we survived washing the mountains of dirty pots and pans at the end of each day. You are amazing! I am lucky to have you as my wife. *Merci pour tout mon pot de miel.*

GURTH

For my wife Deborah, who loves cheese and wine as much as I do.
And for Pinot the Wonder Dog, who is always there to pick up the crumbs.

TONY

TABLE OF CONTENTS

Acknowledgements

Thank you to all the cheesemakers who sent me their delicious cheese, providing me the opportunity to develop yummy recipes for foodies to enjoy.

If Joanne and I ate every portion produced while testing the recipes, my girth would be huge! Thank you to my recipe-tasting Guinea Pig Club, including both sides of the family and my good friends. You know who you are. That is the reason why you were invited to so many meals at our home in such a brief period of time. Not that I do not love you but I needed your appetite and your comments.

To Robert McCullough, my publisher, who believed in the need of my first book *The Definitive Guide to Canadian Artisanal and Fine Cheese*. He saw the importance of a second book, to provide more ideas on how to cook with our delicious Canadian cheese.

An image is worth at least a thousand words. The ones Geoffrey Ross, Ryan Jennings, and Jeff Mayhew created are worth a gazillion. My mouth was watering and my stomach growling when I saw each photograph. Working with you at the studio was an amazing learning experience. Thank you for the great job, guys!

A big thank you to Allison Spurrell of Vancouver's Les Amis du Fromage for providing us with the cheese featured on the book's cover.

And finally a huge thank you to The Bay Co. and Home Outfitters for their support. The plates, glasses, and other table decorations you supplied made the photographs even more gorgeous.

GURTH

I would like to thank all those winemakers across Canada—and around the world—whose wines have made the consumption of cheese in all its forms such a hedonistic pleasure.

TONY

9

Cooking with Cheese
Thoughts from Gurth

My first book, *The Definitive Guide to Canadian Artisanal and Fine Cheese* (Whitecap Books 2006), fuelled readers' appetites to discover and taste our delicious Canadian cheese. With the book in hand, they could explore the world of Canadian cheese. And foodies are doing it!

A cheesemaker informed me that tourists from Ontario stopped at her retail outlet in rural Quebec to buy her cheese. She wondered how they learned of her small artisanal farmstead operation and they showed her my book. They were using it as a Canadian travel and food guide. Hallelujah! My goal of Canadians travelling more in our country, meeting cheesemakers, and learning about local culture is being realized. Experiencing more of what Canada has to offer, meeting Canadians from other provinces, and tasting the local flavours can't help but make us more aware of what a great nation this is. We live in a wonderful country and let's be proud of it! (My patriotic rant is now over.)

This book is the answer to a question I heard many times at events while promoting my first book: "Can you give more ideas and tips on how to cook with cheese?" Cheese is such a versatile ingredient. It can be used in sauces and soups, melted over other ingredients (gratins), added to stuffing, baked—only your imagination restricts your creativity. Have fun, play, experiment, and cook more with cheese.

Canada produces a wonderful variety of cheese. A Camembert-style cheese produced in Quebec will taste different from one made in British Columbia. The influence of the local terroir, or environmental growing conditions, will give each cheese a subtly different flavour from the others. Prepare the recipes with different brands of cheese from across the country and the dish will never taste exactly the same.

Readers also asked if I matched wines to cheese in my first book. Little did they know there are over 1,700 cheese entries in *The Definitive Guide to Canadian Artisanal and Fine Cheese*. If I had suggested wines, the guide might still be in the process of being written. I would be tipsy and very, very, very happy. I asked Tony to complete that portion for this book. He used his great knowledge and experience of wines and other beverages to make suggestions that complement my delicious recipes.

A recipe is a guideline. It provides you with the map to reach your culinary objective. You can easily modify the recipes to your taste and to whatever ingredients you have in your kitchen. Write down the changes you make right on the recipe's page, so you can repeat the outcome when you open this book to prepare the recipe again. However, if you try to modify a baking recipe, be prepared for a different final result. Baking is a science, involving chemical reactions of the ingredients used. You can't replace baking powder with baking soda and expect the cake to rise as well. In this case, you'll have to experiment more to obtain the desired results.

The most important thing is to have fun in the kitchen—and cook more with Canadian cheese!

Santé,

GURTH

Wine with Cheese
Thoughts from Tony

The best cheese and wine match I ever experienced was in Alsace. In a small restaurant outside Colmar I ordered a Munster that had been baked in layers of flaky phyllo pastry. It was sliced birthday cake-style and served warm so the cheese layered throughout the pastry was almost molten. The wine was a chilled glass of Gewurztraminer. I can still remember the combination in my mind's palate—the velvety, rank, salty cheese, the flaky, buttery pastry, and the spicy, aromatic wine of contrasting yet complementary flavour. My mouth waters as I write.

Wine and cheese. Cheese and wine. Almost like love and marriage when the partners are carefully chosen.

There is an old adage in the Bordeaux wine trade that merchants swear by: "Sell on cheese and buy on apples." Try the test for yourself. Take a Granny Smith apple and a slice of mature cheddar. Try them with a glass of any red wine—starting with the apple—and see what happens. Apples, especially Granny Smiths, contain malic acid, which is sour. In fact, winemakers in cool climate regions put their wines through what is called a malolactic fermentation in the spring—a secondary fermentation that converts the sharp malic acid into the softer, less aggressive lactic acid (the acidity you find in milk). If a wine can overcome the malic acid in an apple, it must have lots of concentrated flavour and is therefore a good, marketable wine.

On the other hand, cheese flatters wine. The fat in cheese coats the palate and smoothes out a wine's rough edges, making the tannin in red wines appear more supple and the acidity in whites seem less astringent.

But not all wines go well with all cheeses. There is a commonly held notion that red wines are best with a variety of cheeses whether they're soft, semi-soft, hard, or blue. This misconception was compounded by the fact that most hosts offer the cheese tray after the main course, during which a red wine is most often served. The cheese is meant to "mop up" the remainder of the red wine. But in my experience white wines with light or no oaking are far more compatible with most cheeses.

Charts on pages 22 and 23 set out my recommendations for the kinds of wine to match with a wide range of cheese types. For each of Chef Gurth's delicious recipes I have recommended a range of beverages—wine, fortified wine, beer, spirits, and liqueurs—that will complement or contrast with the flavours in the dish. Some of the best matches pit a salty, savoury cheese dish against a sweet wine (think Stilton and port). But please don't feel constrained to follow any recommendations rigidly. To help you experiment, I have listed the style of wine that pairs most successfully with the dish (for example, a dry, unoaked, medium-bodied white with good acidity, or full-bodied red with a touch of sweetness). Just enjoy.

Cheers!

TONY

A Cheese Primer

To truly appreciate cheese, one must understand the basic facts of cheese production: the major ingredients, the milk terminology, the methods used, and the categories of cheese. With this information in hand, you are ready to have a knowledgeable conversation regarding cheese with your local cheesemonger.

The basic ingredients of cheese are milk, salt, bacterial culture, and a coagulation agent. Other ingredients may be added to give the cheese more flavour and to preserve it longer. The main ingredient, of course, is milk. But there are a number of choices, all of which determine to a large extent the character of the cheese.

Cheese Production

The three steps for making cheese are coagulation, draining, and ripening/ageing.

1 COAGULATION

Milk is transformed into a gelatinous mass called curds. This can occur though acidification via lactic fermentation, adding an enzyme (either animal or vegetable-based), or a combination of both processes.

2 DRAINING

Draining accelerates the drainage of the liquid whey (water and soluble proteins) from the solid curd. It can be done slowly via gravity, mechanically pressed, or cooked and pressed.

3 RIPENING & AGEING

The ripening and ageing of cheese will affect its composition, texture, flavours, aromas, and nutritional value. Time and controllable environmental factors (moisture and temperature) in the ripening facility will assist the enzymes in the cheese to transform the interior paste to creamy and supple, or hard and dry, in texture. Different techniques in treating the cheese will produce different final products. Additional moulds, such as *Penicillium,* may be sprayed onto the rind to create a bloomy type cheese such as brie. Other cheese may have their rinds brushed or washed with saltwater brine or an alcohol. *Penicillium roquefortii* may be injected to form blue cheese. The cheese may also be permitted to age naturally over several years, developing a natural thick rind.

Milk Terminology

COW/DAIRY

Cows are the main milk producers in Canada. Breeds such as Ayrshire, Brown Swiss, Canadienne, and Jersey provide milk high in butterfat and protein. Holstein is the most popular breed amongst dairy farmers, due to the breed's high production volumes. The dairy cow industry is long established in Canada, as compared to raising goats and sheep for milk.

GOAT

Alpine, La Mancha, Laucanne, Nubian, Saanen, and Toggenberg goats are breeds used in Canada for the production of milk. Goat milk can be easier to digest for people who are lactose intolerant. It's a rich milk, used extensively in producing fresh and soft cheese.

SHEEP

East Friesian is the predominant dairy sheep breed in Canada. Raising dairy sheep is a fairly recent phenomenon here. Sheep milk is richer than cow or goat milk and is very nutritious. Similar to goat milk, it is more easily digested by those who are lactose intolerant.

RAW MILK

Canadian laws allow raw milk to be used in the production of cheese. The milk has not been heated over 40°C (104°F) prior to being processed, so all the original bacteria are still present in the milk. Most companies that produce raw-milk cheese obtain their milk from a single supplier or herd. This facilitates monitoring and quality control of the milk. For the cheese to be sold, it must be aged for no less than 60 days. After this date, the potentially harmful bacteria have died off. Among cheese connoisseurs, the flavours provided by the good bacteria produce a complex and subtle cheese.

THERMALIZED MILK

Thermalization of milk occurs when the milk has been heated to a temperature between 57 and 63.5°C (134 and 146°F) for a minimum of 15 seconds prior to being processed into cheese. It's believed this procedure significantly reduces potentially harmful bacteria. The remaining harmful bacteria die during the ageing period. The potential for subtle flavours still exists, depending on the skills of the cheesemaker.

PASTEURIZED MILK

Pasteurization of milk kills all bacteria, good and bad. The milk is either heated to 61.6°C (143°F) for 30 seconds, or to 72–85°C (162–185°F) for 15 seconds. Beneficial bacteria is re-introduced into the milk to begin the cheesemaking process. Most cheese made in Canada is produced using pasteurized milk.

Cheese Categories

FRESH

All cheese begins as fresh, unripened cheese. Those eaten fresh have a high moisture content (up to 80%), as little of the extra whey has been drained. They have a short refrigerated shelf life of up to four weeks.
Examples are cream cheese, cottage cheese, paneer, quark, and ricotta.

SOFT

Fresh curds are placed into moulds and permitted to drain naturally, as soft cheeses have 50–60% moisture content. They may be: unripened, white, and bloomy (due to the addition of *Penicillium* mould); washed with salt water or other liquid; or a combination of both bloomy and washed (that is, mixed). Their refrigerated shelf life is one to two months.
Examples are brie, Camembert, chèvre, and crottin.

SEMI-SOFT

Firmer than the soft cheese (40–60% moisture content), the semi-soft category is divided into several subgroups, depending on how it is ripened.

- **UNRIPENED**   Cheese is cut and stretched after the draining process.
  Examples are bocconcini and mozzarella.
- **INTERIOR RIPENED**   Curds have been pressed, cooked, and ripened. Ripening occurs throughout the whole body of the cheese. Rinds may be washed or brushed.
  Examples are Casata and Monterey Jack.
- **SURFACE RIPENED**   The cheese are turned, washed, and aged in a cold room. Ripening occurs from the surface toward the centre of the cheese.
  Examples are Oka and Limburger.

The refrigerated shelf life of semi-soft cheese is from two to four months.

FIRM

The fresh curds are drained more and heavily pressed to remove more whey (35–45% moisture content). Some cheeses in this category are cooked, making them even firmer. They are all interior ripened. They may be rindless (provolone and cheddar), washed and brushed (Miranda), or covered in wax or plastic (Gouda). Their refrigerated shelf life is three months to a year.

HARD

Hard cheeses are cooked and pressed. They can be aged for a long time. They are used extensively in cooking (gratins) where their sharp flavours are appreciated. They have a very low moisture content (25–35%) and have the longest refrigerated shelf life of over a year.
Examples are chèvretal, Kefalotyri, Leoni-Grana, and Parmesan.

BLUE

Blue in my mind is a true category of cheese. A mould, such as *Penicillium roquefortii*, is introduced onto the rind or inserted into the ageing cheese. This mould produces the blue surface or veining. Blue cheese is mostly produced in the soft and semi-soft categories.
Examples are Lavender Blue, Blossom's Blue, Ciel de Charlevoix, and Chèvre Noit.

Buying & Storing Cheese

BUYING

Purchase from a reputable cheesemonger, one who knows the products, their characteristics, and how to store them properly.

Check the best-before date on the packaging. If uncertain about the taste of a certain cheese, ask for a sample. Remember the sample is not at its best, for the cheese is in a refrigerated display and will be cold.

Purchase only what you need for the next week. Buy cheese to be eaten, not to be forgotten or lost in the refrigerator where it can spoil.

I prefer to have my pieces of cheese cut fresh from the larger wheel or block. Vacuum-wrapped pieces cannot be smelled, nor are you informed as to when the cheese was cut and packaged.

If the cheese you purchased smells of ammonia, return it to the cheesemonger with the receipt. It may be an off cheese, stored improperly during shipment or by the cheesemonger. He or she may offer you a refund or another piece of cheese as a replacement.

STORING

If you are unable to refrigerate cheese immediately, place it in a cooler with ice packs.

Refrigerate wrapped cheese until 90 minutes prior to serving it on a platter.

Cheese should not be rewrapped in its original packaging. It will no longer be airtight and the cheese will deteriorate faster.

Rewrap cheese in fresh wrapping material each time you open it:

- Bloomy rind, mixed rind, and washed rind cheese should be wrapped first in parchment or waxed paper, and then in either plastic wrap or an airtight re-sealable plastic bag. These types of cheese need to breathe, and should be protected from excess moisture. Every second day, turn the cheese over.
- Firm and hard cheese should be rewrapped in plastic wrap or an airtight re-sealable plastic bag. Unwanted moisture is blocked by the layer of plastic.
- Cheese such as a feta, purchased in a saltwater brine solution, should be returned to the original container and its brine solution.
- Blue cheese should be wrapped in foil. This reduces the possibility of its strong aroma infiltrating other ingredients in the refrigerator.

Creating & Serving Cheese Platters

Today there's a renewed interest in serving cheese as a separate course at parties. An old tradition is enjoying a renaissance!

WHEN TO SERVE IT?

Cheese platters can be served at any time of the day or night. They're perfect for a breakfast, brunch buffet, lunch, picnic, tailgate party, dinner, or an after-theatre snack.

At dinner, French Canadians traditionally serve cheese platters before the dessert course. Canadians of British heritage have theirs after the dessert. There are no set rules. Have fun and serve it whenever you want.

Joanne and I love having a cheese platter as our dessert course. I serve it at the end of the meal in the living room, which permits us to leave the dining room and enter a less formal setting. Guests sit where they wish and begin nibbling at the cheese selection. Port, wine, coffee, and tea are offered and the conversations renew. A cheese platter is a great way to end a meal.

PREPARATION

Plan to serve three to four different cheeses on your platter.

Anticipate each guest will eat 100 g (4 oz) of cheese in total. This amount is generous, and there will possibly be some leftovers for a future snack. The actual amount varies according to the individual person, time of day the platter is served, and the social occasion (picnic versus after-dinner cheese platter).

Decide what types of cheese you want to serve. You might have a theme:

- Cheeses made with different kinds of milk (such as cow, goat, and sheep)
- Raw, thermalized, pasteurized cheese
- Cheese representative of different categories (such as soft, semi-soft, firm, hard, bloomy rind, washed rind, blue)
- Local, regional, national, or international cheese

Let the cheese warm up at room temperature, unwrapped, for at least 90 minutes.

Leave the cheese as an entire piece or large pieces. Don't cut it into cubes or small wedges as it will dry out faster. If you cut a double or triple cream too early, the paste will ooze out and spread onto the platter.

Provide a separate knife for each cheese to reduce the chance of cross-contamination of flavours. You don't want a knife that just cut a blue cheese to slice a piece of brie. You will not taste the true flavours of the brie with the small crumbs of the blue transferred by the knife.

Place a card on each cheese to identify it. Your guests will thank you for informing them of the offered selection.

If you're a cheese purist, serve slices of white baguette or water crackers alongside. The neutral base will not compete with the cheese flavours.

Other possibilities are to offer a selection of side garnishes. Roasted garlic, pistachios, caramelized walnuts, fruit chutney, flavoured breads or crackers, and fresh or dried fruit are popular choices. Drizzling artisanal honey over the cheese is becoming very trendy.

Cutting Cheese

Cut cheese in such a way that everyone will be able to sample both the paste and the rind. How you cut it depends on the shape and size of the cheese.

- **FLAVOURED CHÈVRE LOG**
  cut in half lengthwise, then slice into half-moons
- **CAMEMBERT**
  cut into small triangles
- **BRIE**
  cut into thin long points
- **PYRAMID-SHAPED CHEESE**
  cut into tall wedges, from the centre of the cheese
- **OKA**
  cut into wedges
- **CHEDDAR**
  cut into small blocks
- **GOUDA**
  cut into wedges
- **BLUE**
  cut into wedges

There are special cheese knives that make cutting the cheese easier. Some have holes in the blade so the cheese will not stick to the metal. Others have stiff blades able to cut through hard, dry cheese. Visit a specialty cookware store or a good cheesemonger to see a selection of knives.

Fruit Accompaniments

Stay away from citrus fruits when selecting fruit to accompany cheese. The citric acid in oranges and grapefruit is much stronger than the acids in wine. The sharper fruit acid will deaden your perception of the acidity in the wine and make it taste too sweet. Dried fruits go well with cheese—figs, dates, raisins—but you'll need some sweetness in the wine to balance the fruit. In Spain and Portugal they make wonderful marmalade from quince, which works really well with the firm mountain cheeses of those countries.

The all-time best fruit combination with cheese is pear. It's mildly flavoured and doesn't interfere with the flavours in the cheese. Better still, it's light in acid, so it won't make your wine taste flat. Other fruits that go well alongside cheese are strawberries, seedless grapes, and kiwi. Arrange them around your cheese platter as finger food.

If you're serving fruit with cheese, Tony recommends a fortified wine, such as a tawny or ruby port, Oloroso sherry, or Bual Madeira.

A Wine & Cheese Primer

For a successful pairing of wine and cheese, keep in mind the style of the cheese and the character of the wine. The stronger the flavour of the cheese, the sweeter and weightier the wine should be. For powerful cheese like roquefort and Danish blue, go for equally powerful wines like port and sherry. Blue cheese tends to be very salty, and a sweeter wine will cut through that saltiness and refresh your taste buds. White wine generally goes better with creamy cheese (brie and Camembert) than does red. Or you can serve a light chillable red, such as Beaujolais or Valpolicella. The act of chilling brings out the perception of acidity.

Decide whether you want a complementary flavour match (a crisp, dry white wine with a buttery, nutty cheese, for example), or a contrasting flavour match (such as a salty blue cheese with a sweet, round red wine).

Cheese & Wine Pairing Guidelines

Following are some general guidelines using classifications based on how the cheese is made and ripened. For specific pairing suggestions, see the charts on pages 22 and 23.

CHEESE TYPE	CHEESE EXAMPLE	WINE STYLE
FRESH CHEESE Usually white in colour, these cheeses are not fermented and are consumed unripened. The cheese can be salted or unsalted and some have herb flavouring.	• Canadian cottage cheese • cream cheese • quark • ricotta	Dry sparkling or crisp, dry, light-bodied white wines.
SOFT CHEESE These cheeses have a white, bloomy crust, with a soft, spreadable, butter-coloured paste.	• Canadian brie • Camembert • Canadian feta	Dry white or fruity young reds.
SEMI-SOFT CHEESE A large range of products and styles represent this category of cheese, which are somewhat firmer than soft cheese.	• Bocconcini • Mozzarella • havarti • Monterey Jack • Saint-Paulin • Limburger • Oka • Munster	• Gamay • Cabernet blends • Pinot Noir (for highly aromatic cheese like Munster)
HARDER CHEESE These cheeses can be firm or solid. The older they are the harder they become.	• cheddar • Parmesan	Medium to full-bodied dry reds such as Cabernet blends, Barolo/Barbaresco, Shiraz, Zinfandel. The older the cheese, the more full-bodied and flavourful the wine will be.
BLUE CHEESE These can range from creamy as in Dolce Latte to firm. The mould is slightly bitter and the style of cheese a little salty, especially when it is aged.	• Stilton • roquefort	A sweet wine high in alcohol is the best match; try port, sherry, Icewine, Bual, Marsala.

Cheese & Wine Charts

We have an amazing selection of cheese here in Canada, as well as a formidable range of wines, but we have to give credit where credit is due and admit that other countries produce some astounding cheese, to say nothing of wonderful wines. So, in the spirit of international brotherhood, on the following pages we offer two charts: one for matching Canadian wine and cheese, the other for matching cheese from Europe with wine styles from around the world.

Canadian Pairings

CHEESE	WINE STYLE
BOCCONCINI	Gamay Noir, Zweigelt, Pinot Noir
BRICK	Cabernet Franc, Merlot
BRIE	Chardonnay Reserve, Pinot Blanc
BRIE *(double crème)*	Very dry sparkling wine, Auxerrois
BRIE *(triple crème)*	Unoaked Chardonnay, Aligoté, very dry sparkling wine
CAMEMBERT	Chardonnay (barrel-aged), Pinot Gris
CANTONNIER	Chardonnay (medium-bodied), Gamay Noir
CHEDDAR *(mild)*	Chardonnay, Riesling Reserve
CHEDDAR *(old)*	Cabernet Sauvignon blends, Merlot
COLBY	Pinot Noir, Gamay Noir, rosé/light unoaked red
CROTTIN	Chardonnay, Sauvignon Blanc, Pinot Blanc
EMMENTHAL	Auxerrois, dry Riesling, Gamay Noir
ERMITE BLEU	Select Late Harvest Riesling/Late Harvest Vidal, port-style red
FARMERS	Cabernet Franc, Merlot
FETA	Sauvignon Blanc, dry Riesling, dry sparkling
FRIULANO	Chardonnay, Reserve Riesling, Cabernet Sauvignon, Merlot
GOUDA	Pinot Noir, Merlot, Cabernet blends
GRUYÈRE	Riesling, lightly oaked Chardonnay, Cabernet/Merlot blend, Meritage
HAVARTI	Unoaked Chardonnay, Pinot Blanc, Pinot Gris
MARBLE	Chardonnay Reserve, Cabernet blends, Merlot
MONTEREY JACK	Oak-aged Chardonnay, Sauvignon Blanc
OKA	Pinot Noir, Gamay Noir, light reds
PROVOLONE	Baco Noir, Maréchal Foch
RACLETTE	Dry Riesling, Gamay Noir
SAINT-BENOÎT	Oak-aged Chardonnay, Gamay, Merlot
SAINT-PAULIN	Cabernet Sauvignon, Merlot, Cabernet Franc
SWISS	Chardonnay, Cabernet rosé, Gamay
VACHERIN	Dry Riesling, young Cabernet Sauvignon

International Pairings

CHEESE	WINE
ASIAGO	Barolo, Barbaresco, Nebbiolo d'Alba
BRICK	Zinfandel, Côtes du Rhône, California Pinot Noir
BRIE	Sancerre, Frascati/Beaujolais
CAMEMBERT	Burgundy, dry Riesling, Vouvray
CHEDDAR	Rhône, Bordeaux, Burgundy, Zinfandel
CHESHIRE	Beaujolais, Valpolicella, Gamay
CHÈVRE	Sancerre, Pouilly-Fumé
COULOMMIERS	Burgundy, Pinot Noir, Merlot
CROTTIN	Chablis, Sancerre
DANISH BLUE	Oloroso sherry, Sauternes/Late Bottled Vintage port
EDAM	Beaujolais, Valpolicella, Gamay
EMMENTHAL	Mâcon Blanc, Riesling
ÉPOISSE	Marc de Bourgogne, grappa
FETA	Greek whites, Pouilly-Fumé, Fumé Blanc
GORGONZOLA	Amarone, Late Harvest Zinfandel, ruby port
GOUDA	Rioja, red Burgundy, Oregon Pinot Noir
GRUYÈRE	Rhône white, Chilean Chardonnay/Chinon
HAVARTI	Frascati, Fendant, Muscadet
MASCARPONE	German Riesling, Müller-Thurgau, dry Muscat
MONTEREY JACK	Chardonnay, white Rhône/red Burgundy
MOZZARELLA	Chianti, Barbera, Beaujolais
MUNSTER	Alsace Gewurztraminer, dry Muscat
PARMIGIANO	Valpolicella, Bardolino, Chianti
PONT L'ÉVÊQUE	Côtes de Roussillon, Zinfandel, Montepulciano d'Abruzzo
PORT-SALUT	Rhône white, New Zealand Sauvignon Blanc, Chardonnay
REBLOCHON	Chablis, Muscadet, Soave
ROQUEFORT	Sauternes, Monbazillac/Recioto/port
TÊTE DE MOINE	Frascati, Fendant, Vernaccia di San Gimignano

Roasted Garlic & Double Cheddar Bread, *page 26*

BRUNCH

Roasted Garlic & Double Cheddar Bread

(pictured on page 24)

**Using Old Orange Cheddar, produced by Forfar Dairy Ltd. in Forfar, ON;
and Old White Cheddar, produced by Farmers Cooperative Dairy Ltd. in Truro, NS.**

This recipe combines two of my favourite aromas: roasting garlic and freshly baked bread. They provide me with such a feeling of home comfort. Joanne has declared this bread recipe as her favourite. Many people believe baking your own bread takes so much time. This recipe takes nearly 4 hours to complete, but for 3 of those hours you are not involved. You don't have to watch the dough rise or bake, although you can if you want to. I like to start my loaves in the morning, so that by lunchtime, they are out of the oven and the aroma floats on the air for the rest of the day. I began baking my own bread when Jurgen, an old roommate of mine at Point Pelee National Park, taught me how simple it is. Many loaves of bread have since been baked, with many interesting experiences. I find baking my own bread very therapeutic. While kneading the dough, my mind roams as my body follows the set rhythm of push the dough, quarter-turn, push the dough again, repeat.

2	bulbs garlic, cloves separated (unpeeled)
2	Tbsp (30 mL) extra virgin olive oil
4	cups (1 L) whole wheat bread flour
1	Tbsp (15 mL) quick-rising yeast
½	tsp (2 mL) kosher salt
¼	tsp (1 mL) freshly ground black pepper
1	+ ⅔ cups (400 mL) warm water
5	oz (125 g) Old White Cheddar, shredded
5	oz (125 g) Old Orange Cheddar, shredded

TONY'S SUGGESTIONS
- **FULL-BODIED WHITE WINE**
  White Burgundy, Ontario Chardonnay, dry Sauvignon Blanc
- **ROSÉ**
  Bandol or Tavel
- **BEER**
  Belgian

MAKE AHEAD
- *Garlic cloves can be roasted 2 days ahead, covered, and refrigerated.*

GURTH'S NOTES
- *Have fun and experiment with other firm melting cheese, such as Gouda, Swiss, brick, colby, or farmer's.*

Cooking Instructions

1. **PREHEAT** the oven to 325°F (160°C) and place the oven rack in the centre position.

2. **IN A BOWL,** toss the garlic cloves with the oil. Spread the cloves on a baking sheet and roast for 30 to 40 minutes, or until they're soft and golden.

3. **REMOVE** the garlic from the oven and allow to cool. Once cooled, peel the papery skin off the cloves.

4. **IN A LARGE BOWL,** combine the flour and yeast. Make a well in the centre. Sprinkle the salt and pepper along the top of the well.

5. **POUR** the warm water into the centre of the well, mix until all the ingredients bind together. Add a little more warm water if it's too dry.

6. **ON A LIGHTLY FLOURED WORK SURFACE,** knead the dough for 15 minutes. To knead, push down on the dough with the heels of your hands, then turn it a quarter-turn and push again. Keep repeating this process until the dough feels smooth and elastic. Form the dough into a ball.

7. **COAT** a large bowl with oil. Place the dough in the bowl, rotate to oil the top, and cover with plastic wrap. Let rise in a draft-free area for 45 to 60 minutes or until the dough has doubled in size.

8. **REMOVE** the plastic wrap and punch down the dough.

9. **SET** the oven temperature to 350°F (180°C). Spray a rectangular loaf pan with cooking oil.

10. **ON A LIGHTLY FLOURED WORK SURFACE,** press the dough into a round that's ½ inch (1 cm) thick. Cover with a tea towel and let rest for 20 minutes.

11. **PLACE** half of the roasted garlic at the edge of the dough and begin to roll up the dough toward the other edge.

12. **WHEN THE GARLIC HAS BEEN ROLLED** into the dough, place ⅔ of the white cheddar along the edge of the roll. Continue to roll the dough, enclosing the white cheddar.

13. **WHEN THE WHITE CHEDDAR HAS BEEN ROLLED** into the dough, place ⅔ of the orange cheddar and the remaining garlic along the edge of the roll. Continue to roll the dough to the end.

14. **TUCK** in the ends and place in the loaf pan. Cover with a tea towel and let rise in a draft-free area for 45 to 60 minutes, or until doubled in size.

15. **WITH A SHARP KNIFE,** make a 1-inch-deep (2.5-cm) slash lengthwise on the top of the loaf. Sprinkle the remaining grated cheese overtop.

16. **BAKE** in the preheated oven for 40 to 50 minutes, or until the bread sounds hollow when tapped on the bottom when removed from the pan.

17. **PLACE** the bread on a rack and cool to room temperature before slicing.

Breakfast Polenta
with Italian Sausage & Queso Fresco

Using Queso Fresco, produced by Portuguese Cheese Co. in Toronto, ON.

Chef Tony de Luca of Niagara-on-the-Lake told me years ago he ate polenta for breakfast as a child in Italy. Adding the sausage and cheese entices me to eat this classic dish more often.

1	+ ½ cups (375 mL) Queso Fresco
4	cups (1 L) water
1	lb (500 g) frozen yellow corn kernels
1	cup (250 mL) fine cornmeal
½	tsp (2 mL) chili flakes
1	lb (500 g) mild Italian sausage, casings removed
1	lb (500 g) cherry tomatoes

Cooking Instructions

1 **CRUMBLE** the cheese into a small bowl and set aside.

2 **IN A LARGE SAUCEPAN,** bring the water to a boil and add the frozen corn. Return to a boil.

3 **WHISKING CONSTANTLY,** add the cornmeal in a steady, thin stream. Reduce the temperature to medium-low.

4 **STIR** with a wooden spoon until the polenta has thickened, approximately 5 to 10 minutes. Add the chili flakes. Set aside.

5 **IN A LARGE, HEAVY SKILLET** over medium heat, brown the sausage, breaking the meat into smaller pieces with a wooden spoon, about 6 minutes.

6 **ADD** the cherry tomatoes to the skillet. Cover, reduce the heat to medium, and simmer until the tomatoes soften.

7 **SPOON** the polenta onto individual plates. Top with the cheese and sausage mixture.

TONY'S SUGGESTIONS
- **FULL-BODIED WHITE WINE**
  New World Chardonnay, Alsace Pinot Gris
- **MEDIUM-BODIED RED WINE**
  New World Merlot, Pinot Noir
- **BEER**
  Real ale

MAKE AHEAD
- *This dish is so quick and easy there's nothing you can make ahead.*

GURTH'S NOTES
- *Use your favourite sausages, mild or hot, Italian, German, whatever you are in the mood for.*
- *A mild feta or fresh cheddar curds would be tasty substitutes for the cheese.*

Cheddar Bacon Waffles

Using Medium Cheddar, produced by Laiterie Chalifoux Inc./Fromages Riviera in Sorel/Tracy, QC.

At first, Joanne was a little skeptical about this recipe idea. She loves our homemade waffles but was uncertain about adding the flavour combination of cheese and bacon. I crumbled the cheddar instead of shredding it so there would suddenly be a major burst of cheese flavour when biting into a forkful of the waffle. After a few bites, Joanne was a happy convert.

2	cups (500 mL) pastry flour
2	tsp (10 mL) baking powder
½	tsp (2 mL) baking soda
½	tsp (2 mL) kosher salt
3	oz (75 g) Medium Cheddar, crumbled
2	Tbsp (30 mL) unsalted butter, melted
1	+ ½ cups (375 mL) milk
2	eggs, beaten
2	slices bacon, cooked and diced

TONY'S SUGGESTIONS
- CRISP, DRY WHITE WINE
  Unoaked Chardonnay, Chablis, Muscadet
- FRUITY, ACIDIC RED WINE
  Beaujolais, Ontario or BC Gamay Noir, Valpolicella
- BEER
  English bitter

MAKE AHEAD
- *Cook the bacon ahead of time. Refrigerate.*

GURTH'S NOTES
- *Every time you make this recipe, try a more aged cheddar.*

Cooking Instructions

1 **IN A LARGE BOWL,** sift the flour with the baking powder and soda. Add the salt and crumbled cheese.
2 **IN A SMALLER BOWL,** combine the butter, milk, eggs, and diced bacon.
3 **ADD** the wet ingredients to the dry ingredients and stir just to combine.
4 **COOK** the batter according to the waffle iron manufacturer's directions.
5 **ENJOY** with a pat of melting butter and copious amounts of maple syrup.

Avocado & Lavender Blue Brunch Crostini

Using Lavender Blue, produced by Milky Way Farms in Shelburne, ON.

Joanne and I enjoy eating different breakfast or brunch items. I like surprising her and her taste buds! I believe diversity is the spice of life, especially regarding food. This tasty treat also makes a good hors d'oeuvre.

1	ripe avocado, mashed
1	Tbsp (15 mL) finely sliced green onion
1	oz (25 g) Lavender Blue, diced
1	Tbsp (15 mL) diced red bell pepper
4	slices baguette
1	clove garlic, halved

Cooking Instructions

1 **IN A SMALL BOWL,** combine the avocado, green onion, cheese, and red pepper.

2 **GRILL** the baguette slices on a preheated barbecue or grill pan. Rub the garlic onto 1 side of the grilled baguette.

3 **SPREAD** the avocado/cheese mixture onto the garlic crostini.

4 **SERVE** immediately and watch them disappear!

TONY'S SUGGESTIONS
- DRY WHITE WINE WITH GOOD FRUIT
  New Zealand Sauvignon Blanc, Kabinett-style Riesling, French Viognier
- BEER
  Lager

MAKE AHEAD
- *Stir 1 Tbsp (15 mL) of fresh lime juice into the avocado mixture. Cover with plastic wrap, making sure it sits right on the surface, and refrigerate.*
- *This recipe can be made a day ahead. The juice will help reduce the chance of the avocado oxidizing and turning brown.*
- *Crostini can be grilled a day ahead.*

GURTH'S NOTES
- *Use your favourite crumbly blue cheese, such as Highland Blue, Benedictine Blue, Stilton, or roquefort.*

Black Truffle Cheese Omelette
with Julienne of Carrots, Celery & Leeks

Using Black Truffle Cheese, produced by Bothwell Cheese Inc. in New Bothwell, MB.

When Jason Wortzman of Bothwell Cheese told me about their newly developed Black Truffle Cheese, my mind began filling with recipe ideas. Soufflés, raclette, and omelettes are a few of the delicious possibilities. The aroma of the black truffle cheese as it melts in the omelette makes this dish a favourite for both Joanne and me.

1	Tbsp + 2 tsp (25 mL) extra virgin olive oil
4	baby carrots, julienned
½	celery stalk, peeled, cut into quarters widthwise, and julienned
¼	leek, white parts only, halved lengthwise and julienned
6	eggs, lightly beaten
¼	cup (60 mL) 35% cream
3	oz (75 g) Black Truffle Cheese, shredded

Cooking Instructions

1 **IN A LARGE SKILLET,** heat 1 Tbsp (15 mL) of the oil over medium heat.

2 **ADD** the carrots, celery, and leeks; cook, stirring frequently, until tender. Transfer the vegetables to a plate.

3 **IN A MEDIUM BOWL,** beat the eggs with the cream.

4 **POUR** 1 tsp (5 mL) of the remaining oil into the same skillet and place over medium heat.

5 **WHEN THE OIL IS HOT,** pour ½ of the egg mixture into the skillet. Cook for 5 to 7 minutes, or until the top is nearly set.

6 **PLACE** ½ of the cooked vegetables and shredded cheese on half of the omelette.

7 **FOLD** the other half of the omelette overtop and serve.

8 **REPEAT** steps 4 to 7 for the second omelette.

TONY'S SUGGESTIONS
- FINE ITALIAN RED WINE
  (To match the truffle flavour)
  Barbaresco, Barolo, red
  Burgundy, Ontario Pinot Noir
- BEER *Bock*

MAKE AHEAD
- *Vegetables can be cooked a day ahead, covered, and refrigerated. Bring to room temperature prior to serving.*
- *Egg mixture can be prepared a day ahead, covered, and refrigerated.*

GURTH'S NOTES
- *Use Canadian Edam, Esrom, or flavoured havarti as a substitute for Black Truffle Cheese.*

Cheddar Scones
with Green Onions

Using Le Cru du clocher cheddar, produced by Le Fromage au Village in Lorrainville, QC.

Le Cru du clocher is a raw milk cheddar produced in the Abitibi-Témiscamingue region of northwestern Quebec. Many Canadians believe it's illegal to make and sell raw milk cheese in our country. But government legislation states that as long as the cheese is aged for a minimum of 60 days, the cheese is safe for sale. The potentially harmful bacteria in the milk will have died by the end of this wait period. Seek out raw milk cheese produced in your vicinity and try them. These scones are a great treat, whether with a bowl of soup or stew, or as part of an afternoon tea.

2	+ ¼ cups (560 mL) all-purpose flour
2	Tbsp (30 mL) granulated sugar
2	+ ½ tsp (12 mL) baking powder
½	tsp (2 mL) baking soda
½	tsp (2 mL) kosher salt
½	cup (125 mL) cold unsalted butter, cubed
1	cup (250 mL) shredded Le Cru du clocher cheddar
1	cup (250 mL) milk
1	Tbsp (15 mL) white vinegar
3	green onions, sliced
1	egg, lightly beaten with 1 Tbsp (15 mL) cold water

TONY'S SUGGESTIONS
- **MEDIUM-BODIED, DRY WHITE WINE**
  white Burgundy, Ontario Chardonnay
- **RED WINE**
  Rhône Villages, New World Pinot Noir
- **BEER**
  Brown ale, India Pale Ale

MAKE AHEAD
- *This recipe is so quick and easy, there is nothing you can make ahead.*

GURTH'S NOTES
- *Add a pinch of cayenne or chili flakes to the dry ingredients to give just a hint of heat.*
- *Substitute with your favourite aged cheddar, Colby, or Monterey Jack.*

Cooking Instructions

1 **PREHEAT** the oven to 425°F (220°C) and place the oven rack in the middle position.

2 **IN A LARGE BOWL,** sift the flour, sugar, baking powder, baking soda, and salt.

3 **ADD** the butter. Using 2 butter knives or a pastry cutter, cut the butter into the flour until the mixture resembles coarse crumbs.

4 **STIR** in the cheese. Form a well in the centre of the mixture.

5 **IN A MEASURING CUP,** combine the milk and vinegar. Stir in the green onions.

6 **POUR** the liquid mixture into the centre of the well. Mix the liquids quickly with the dry ingredients. Do not overmix.

7 **ON A LIGHTLY FLOURED** work surface, gently knead the dough 12 times and flatten to ½ inch (1 cm) thickness.

8 **USE** a floured 3-inch (8-cm) biscuit cutter to cut the dough into circles; place on an ungreased baking sheet. Gently re-form the remaining dough into a ball with no seams and flatten it again. Cut more circles with the cutter.

9 **BRUSH** the tops of the scones with the egg mixture.

10 **BAKE** in the preheated oven for 12 to 15 minutes, or until golden in colour.

11 **REMOVE** from the oven and cool on a rack for 5 minutes before they are snatched away and magically disappear.

PREPARATION TIME 30 MINS
 + 1 HR REFRIGERATION
COOKING TIME 45 MINS
MAKES 5–6 SERVINGS

Leek, Borgonzola & Montasio Soufflé

**Using Borgonzola, produced by Quality Cheese Inc. in Vaughan, ON;
and Montasio, produced by Paron Cheese Company Ltd. in Hannon, ON.**

A soufflé is such a crowd pleaser. It is light and flavourful and brings a sense of mystery and awe with it to the table: when will it start to fall? Many believe it is hard to make, but it's actually quite simple. Joanne watched me making it for her and was amazed how easy it was. Should I cross my fingers, hoping one day she will surprise me with one she made herself? Joanne surprises me often with her delicious creations. I am so lucky!

½	cup + 2 Tbsp (155 mL) unsalted butter
1	oz (25 g) Montasio, finely grated
1	Tbsp (15 mL) extra virgin olive oil
2	leeks, white parts only, washed, quartered, thinly sliced
⅓	cup (75 mL) all-purpose flour
1	cup + 2 Tbsp (280 mL) milk
9	oz (225 g) Borgonzola, rind removed, cut into smaller pieces
½	tsp (2 mL) kosher salt
¼	tsp (1 mL) freshly ground black pepper
4	egg yolks, lightly beaten
7	egg whites, beaten to soft peaks

Cooking instructions continued on following page . . .

TONY'S SUGGESTIONS
- **SPARKLING**
  Champagne
- **DRY WHITE WINE**
  Sauvignon Blanc from the Loire (Sancerre, Pouilly-Fumé) or Ontario, unoaked Chardonnay, Soave

MAKE AHEAD
- *Soufflé mould can be dusted with Montasio. The leeks can be cooked 2 days ahead, covered, and refrigerated.*

GURTH'S NOTES
- *Substitute other hard cheese, such as Pecorino, Parmesan, and Old Bra for the Montasio. Italian Gorgonzola or German Cambozola cheese can be used instead of the Borgonzola.*

Leek, Borgonzola & Montasio Soufflé *(continued)*
Cooking Instructions

1 **IN A SMALL SAUCEPAN,** melt the butter over medium-low heat. Skim the white scum off the melted butter.

2 **BRUSH** the inside of an 8-cup (2-L) tall soufflé mould with the melted butter.

3 **DUST** ½ of the Montasio cheese onto the buttered surfaces. Chill the mould in the refrigerator for 30 minutes.

4 **REPEAT** steps 2 and 3 with more melted butter and the remaining Montasio.

5 **PREHEAT** the oven to 400°F (200°C) and place the oven rack in the second-lowest position.

6 **IN A MEDIUM SKILLET,** heat the oil over medium-low temperature. Add the leeks, cover, and cook until softened, about 5 to 7 minutes. Set aside to cool.

7 **POUR** the remaining melted butter into a large saucepan and place over medium heat. Stir in the flour and cook for 3 minutes.

8 **DRIZZLE** the milk into the flour mixture, whisking well to ensure no lumps form. Continue to cook and whisk until a thick sauce forms, about 5 minutes.

9 **ADD** the cooled leeks, Borgonzola cheese, salt, and pepper and stir until the cheese has melted.

10 **REMOVE** the saucepan from the heat and allow to cool for 3 minutes.

11 **GRADUALLY STIR** in the egg yolks.

12 **GENTLY** fold the egg whites into the mixture, keeping it light and fluffy.

13 **POUR** the soufflé mixture into the prepared mould and place on a baking sheet.

14 **BAKE** in the preheated oven for 5 minutes, then lower the temperature to 325°F (160°C) and continue to cook for 20 minutes. Do not open the oven door or the soufflé may collapse. Remove the mould from the oven and bring the soufflé straight to the table for all your guests to admire and enjoy.

PREPARATION TIME 10 MINS
COOKING TIME 25 MINS
MAKES 4 SERVINGS

Spicy Topless Coddled Eggs

Using Chèvrai, produced by Woolwich Dairy Inc. in Orangeville, ON.

As a memento of their first visit to England, my parents brought back with them two small ceramic egg cups with lids you could screw onto them. My dad demonstrated how to make coddled eggs several times. He thought I was a slow learner. Unbeknownst to him at the time, I was a smart young lad, getting others to prepare breakfast for me.

8	eggs, lightly beaten
½	cup (125 mL) 35% cream
2	oz (50 g) Chèvrai, crumbled
4	green onions, finely sliced
4	tsp (20 mL) diced hot banana peppers

Cooking Instructions

1. **PREHEAT** the oven to 350°F (180°C) and place the oven rack in the centre position.
2. **IN A MIXING BOWL**, combine all the ingredients.
3. **SPRAY** four 1-cup (250-mL) ramekins with cooking oil.
4. **DIVIDE** the mixture between the ramekins.
5. **BRING** 5 cups (1.25 L) of water to a boil.
6. **PLACE** a tea towel in a small roasting pan. Put the ramekins on top of the tea towel. Pour the hot water into the roasting pan; the water should come halfway up the sides of the ramekins.
7. **BAKE** in the preheated oven for 25 minutes.
8. **CAREFULLY REMOVE** the ramekins from the roasting pan and place on individual plates to serve.

TONY'S SUGGESTIONS
- **DRY SPARKLING WINE**
  preferably champagne
- **UNOAKED WHITE WINE**
  Unoaked Chardonnay, dry Riesling
- **BEER**
  Pale Ale

MAKE AHEAD
- *Mixture can be prepared a day ahead, covered, and refrigerated.*

GURTH'S NOTES
- *The centre will be runny, which is great if you enjoy dipping strips of buttered toast into them. If you want the eggs to be set in the middle, cook for an extra 5 minutes.*
- *If you like things spicier, add extra banana peppers.*
- *Use any soft, fresh goat cheese. Flavoured goat cheese would be tasty too.*

Croque Bûcheron

Using Lotbinière, produced by Fromagerie Bergeron in Saint-Antoine-de-Tilly, QC.

After an overnight flight to Paris from Toronto, Joanne and I were a little jet-lagged and seriously hungry. Airline food still has a long way to go to be classified as a gastronomical experience. Our first meal at a Paris café included a Croque Monsieur and a Croque Madame, the classic open-faced sandwiches, with a glass of wine, of course. (Why does the Madame have the sunny-side-up egg on top of the melted cheese?) I'm the hungry one. I want two eggs on mine, as if I was a hungry bûcheron (lumberjack). Monty Python's famous lumberjack song pops into my head: "I'm a lumberjack and I'm okay. I sleep all night and I work all day. I cut down trees, I eat my lunch . . ." This dish would be a light snack for a hearty bûcheron, who would probably eat several at one sitting.

12	slices peameal bacon
1	loaf multi-grain bread (unsliced)
12	slices Lotbinière cheese
4	Tbsp (60 mL) unsalted butter
12	eggs

TONY'S SUGGESTIONS
- **MEDIUM-BODIED, DRY RED WINE**
  Pinot Noir (red Burgundy, New World Pinot Noir), Beaujolais, Gamay
- **FORTIFIED WINE**
  Oloroso sherry

GURTH'S NOTES
- *Use your favourite style of melting cheese instead, such as raclette, Héritage, Monterey Jack, mozzarella, Gouda.*
- *If you can't get your hands on peameal bacon, use smoked ham, maple-cured bacon, or sliced dried sausages.*

Cooking Instructions

1 **SET** the oven to broil and place an oven rack at the second-highest level.

2 **IN A LARGE SKILLET** over medium heat, cook the bacon for 2 to 3 minutes, browning both sides and cooking in batches, if necessary. Transfer the cooked bacon to a paper-lined cookie sheet.

3 **CUT** the loaf of bread into 4 lengthwise slices. Place the slices on a cookie sheet and broil until lightly golden. Flip the slices over to brown the other side. Set aside.

4 **ARRANGE** the bacon on the toasted bread. Cover with the cheese slices.

5 **PLACE** the same skillet over medium heat, melt 1 Tbsp (15 mL) of the butter, and fry 3 eggs without breaking the yolks. Cook until the egg whites have set.

6 **PLACE** the cookie sheet with 1 croque bûcheron under the broiler until the cheese begins to turn gold and bubbles. Remove from the oven.

7 **SET** the cooked eggs on top of the melted cheese.

8 **REPEAT** steps 5 to 7 for the remaining 3 slices of bread.

9 **SERVE** hot and eat before another hungry bûcheron gobbles it up.

Smoked Salmon
with Herb & Garlic Chèvre Panini

Using Herb and Garlic Chèvre from Mariposa Dairy, produced in Oakwood, ON.

Some days, Joanne and I are just not in the mood to cook. A good grilled panini sandwich with a salad or a previously made soup is the perfect solution. This is especially true when it includes smoked salmon, one of Joanne's favourite ingredients. This dish can be enjoyed at any meal: breakfast, brunch, lunch, or dinner.

⅓	wholegrain baguette
4	Tbsp (60 mL) Herb & Garlic Chèvre, at room temperature
½	tsp (2 mL) lemon zest
2	large green lettuce leaves
4	slices Atlantic smoked salmon
1	green onion, finely sliced
2	Tbsp (30 mL) capers, drained
1	Tbsp (15 mL) unsalted butter, at room temperature

TONY'S SUGGESTIONS
- MEDIUM-BODIED, CRISPLY DRY WHITE WINE
  Sauvignon Blanc from the Loire Valley (Sancerre, Pouilly-Fumé), Mosel Riesling QbA, Muscadet
- FORTIFIED WINE
  Fino or Manzanilla sherry
- BEER
  Pale ale, lager

MAKE AHEAD
- *Sandwich can be assembled 4 hours ahead, covered, and refrigerated. Grill just before serving.*

GURTH'S NOTES
- *For a different flavour experience, use a black peppercorn or garlic-flavoured goat or soft sheep cheese.*

Cooking Instructions

1 **PREHEAT** your panini grill to maximum.

2 **REMOVE** the top crust of the baguette and cut the remainder into 4 slices lengthwise. Spread the chèvre cheese evenly on the top of the bottom slice and the bottom of the top slice.

3 **SPRINKLE** the bottom slice with ½ of the lemon zest and cover with a leaf of lettuce.

4 **COVER** the bottom slice with the second slice of bread. Place 2 slices of smoked salmon on top. Spread ½ the green onions and capers over the salmon.

5 **COVER** with the third slice of bread and repeat with the remaining salmon, onions, and capers.

6 **PLACE** the remaining lettuce leaf and lemon zest atop the salmon/onions mixture; cover with the top slice of bread, cheese-side down.

7 **SPREAD** the softened butter over the top of the sandwich; place in the hot panini grill and cook until grill marks appear and the cheese is just starting to melt.

8 **REMOVE** the sandwich from the grill and cut in half crosswise before serving.

Kielbasa Strata

Using Qualicum Spice, produced by Little Qualicum Cheeseworks in Parksville, BC.

In our neighbourhood, there are many small Eastern European delicatessens. Joanne and I both love walking into them, smelling the smoke-cured meats, and hearing the staff speaking Polish or Ukrainian with the other customers. The nearest deli sells a very tasty garlic-flavoured kielbasa. We enjoy buying the occasional chunk as part of our weekend treat

½   loaf French bread, cut into 1-inch (2 ½-cm) cubes

4   oz (100 g) kielbasa, cut into 1-inch (2 ½-cm) cubes

½   cup (125 mL) chopped green onions

6   oz (150 g) Qualicum Spice cheese, shredded

2   cups (500 mL) milk

6   eggs, beaten

½   tsp (2 mL) dry mustard

½   tsp (2 mL) kosher salt

•   pinch of freshly ground black pepper

1   cup (250 mL) 35% cream

½   tsp (2 mL) freshly grated nutmeg

TONY'S SUGGESTIONS
- **FRUITY, YOUNG RED WINE**
  Beaujolais, Valpolicella, Ontario/BC Pinot Noir
- **DRY ROSÉ**
  Tavel or Bandol
- **OFF-DRY WHITE**
  Riesling, Gewurztraminer
- **BEER**
  Dark lager

MAKE AHEAD
- *Make it the night before you plan to eat it for brunch.*

GURTH'S NOTES
- *Try using different breads: day-old croissants, sourdough, or rye.*
- *Use Munster, Limburger, or other flavoured cheese.*

Cooking Instructions

1   **SPRAY** an 8-inch (2-L) baking dish with cooking oil.

2   **LAYER** the bread, kielbasa, green onions, and ½ of the cheese in the dish.

3   **IN** a bowl, beat the milk, eggs, dry mustard, salt, and pepper together.

4   **POUR** the egg mixture over the bread/kielbasa mixture.

5   **SPRINKLE** the remaining cheese on top. Cover and refrigerate overnight.

6   **PREHEAT** the oven to 375°F (190°C) and place the oven rack in the centre position.

7   **MIX** the cream and nutmeg together and pour over the strata.

8   **BAKE** in the oven for 50 to 60 minutes, or until golden.

9   **REMOVE** from the oven and let cool for 10 minutes before serving.

Toad in a Montreal Pothole

Using Garden Vegetable Havarti, produced by Agropur in Montreal, QC.

There are two things that I believe set my native city of Montreal apart from any other in Canada—our sweet and chewy bagels and the city's inexhaustible number of street potholes. Often when I meet ex-Montrealers, I ask them which is their favourite bagel bakery in the city. If they state St-Viateur, then a potential friendship is in the making; any other and it's iffy. Fresh bagels are a great snack after leaving the city's nightclubs on Bishop and Crescent streets at 3 a.m. When the sesame or poppy seed-coated bagels are fresh out of the wood-burning oven, no butter, cream cheese, or lox is required. I decided to have fun with the classic toad-in-a-hole recipe and create my version, dedicating it to my hometown.

3	Tbsp (45 mL) extra virgin olive oil
1	large Spanish onion, halved and sliced
2	leeks, white parts only, sliced
5	cremini mushrooms, sliced
1	cup (250 mL) baby spinach, sliced into thin strips
2	bagels, sliced and toasted
4	eggs
12	slices Garden Vegetable Havarti (3 oz/75 g)

TONY'S SUGGESTIONS
- **WHITE WINE**
  Alsace Pinot Blanc, lightly oaked Ontario/BC Chardonnay, Sauvignon Blanc
- **RED WINE**
  Pinot Noir
- **CIDER**
  Dry

MAKE AHEAD
- *Caramelized onions and mushroom/spinach mixture can be prepared and cooked 2 days ahead, covered, and refrigerated. Bring to room temperature before serving.*

GURTH'S NOTES
- *Use other good melting cheese, like Munster, Monterey Jack, or mozzarella.*

Cooking Instructions

1 **PREHEAT** the oven to 325°F (160°C) and place the oven rack in the centre position. Spray a baking sheet with cooking oil.

2 **IN A LARGE SKILLET,** heat 2 Tbsp (30 mL) of the oil over medium-low temperature. Add the sliced onion and cook until soft and golden, 20 to 30 minutes. Remove the skillet from the heat and set aside.

3 **IN A MEDIUM SKILLET,** heat the remaining 1 Tbsp (15 mL) of oil over medium temperature. Cook the leeks and mushrooms for 5 minutes, or until softened.

4 **ADD** the spinach and cook for 2 minutes. Remove from the heat and set aside.

5 **PLACE** the toasted bagels on the baking sheet.

6 **DIVIDE** the caramelized onions among the bagel halves, filling the holes with the mixture.

7 **COVER** with the mushroom/spinach mixture and form a well in the centre, creating a small nest.

8 **CRACK** an egg in the centre of each nest and cover with 3 slices of cheese.

9 **BAKE** in the preheated oven for 20 minutes, or until the whites are set and the yolks are still soft.

Grilled Pork Tenderloin Sandwich with Double Crème Brie, *page 50*

LUNCH

Grilled Vegetable Pizza

Using Le Diable aux vaches, produced by Les Fromages de l'Érablière Inc. in Mont-Laurier, QC.

Another of Joanne's favourite dishes is my homemade pizza. We use whatever we have in the fridge. Substitute any vegetables you like and use your own sauce or a store-bought version. In less time than it takes to order and receive a pizza from your local pizzeria, you can have a customized pizza that's just the way you like it. I like buying fresh pizza dough either from a pizzeria or from a grocery store. I find fresh dough has a nicer texture than one that has thawed.

½	eggplant, sliced and salted for 60 minutes
6	Tbsp (90 mL) canola oil
1	red onion, sliced
2	small zucchini, sliced lengthwise
1	ball store-bought pizza dough
4	Tbsp (60 mL) pizza sauce
4	oz (100 g) Le Diable aux vaches cheese, rind removed and sliced
½	cup (125 mL) olives, pitted and sliced

TONY'S SUGGESTIONS

- **DRY RED WINE**
  Chianti, Valpolicella, Barbera, Sangiovese, Ontario/BC Pinot Noir or Gamay
- **DRY WHITE WINE**
  New Zealand Sauvignon Blanc, Grüner Veltliner, Chablis
- **BEER**
  Italian, amber ale

MAKE AHEAD
- *The vegetables can be grilled 1 day ahead, covered, and refrigerated.*

GURTH'S NOTES
- *Try raclette, La Barre du Jour, Oka, or any semi-soft, washed rind cheese.*

Cooking Instructions

1 **PREHEAT** the oven to 350°F (180°C) and place the rack in the centre position.
2 **RINSE** the eggplant slices and pat them dry.
3 **PREHEAT** a barbecue or grill pan to medium-high.
4 **PLACE** the oil and eggplant in a large bowl and stir to coat the slices with oil.
5 **GRILL** the eggplant for 3 to 4 minutes on both sides, or until soft. Transfer to a plate and set aside.
6 **COAT** the onion slices with the oil and grill until soft and slightly caramelized, about 3 to 5 minutes. Transfer to a plate and set aside.
7 **COAT** the zucchini slices with the oil and grill on both sides until they are soft and grill marks appear, about 2 minutes per side. Transfer to a plate and set aside.
8 **DUST** your work surface with flour. Roll out the pizza dough and fit it into a large round pizza pan.
9 **SPREAD** the sauce over the dough and arrange the grilled vegetables on top.
10 **ARRANGE** the cheese and olives overtop.
11 **BAKE** in the preheated oven for 20 to 25 minutes.
12 **REMOVE** from the oven and devour immediately.

PREPARATION TIME 10 MINS
COOKING TIME 8 MINS
MAKES 2 SERVINGS

Grilled Pork Tenderloin Sandwich
with Double Crème Brie *(pictured on page 46)*

Using Double Crème Brie, produced by La Fromagerie Alexis de Portneuf Inc. in Saint-Raymond-de-Portneuf, QC.

I am always looking for ways to use our delicious Canadian pork. It is so lean that it can be cooked medium-rare, still rosy pink in the centre. Mentioning this little-known fact makes my good friend Bruce Thompson, Chef and Nutritionist for Ontario Pork, happy: it's something he has been informing the food service industry and consumers about for many years.

1	Tbsp (15 mL) unsalted butter
2	pieces pork tenderloin, 3 oz (75 g) each
•	kosher salt and freshly ground black pepper, to taste
2	Tbsp (30 mL) Dijon mustard
2	onion buns, halved and grilled
2	Tbsp (30 mL) aioli
2	Tbsp (30 mL) diced roasted red peppers
8	arugula leaves
2	radicchio leaves
6	slices Double Crème Brie

Cooking Instructions

1 **IN A SMALL SKILLET,** heat the butter over medium-high temperature.

2 **SEASON** the pork with salt and pepper, and cook for 4 minutes on each side.

3 **TRANSFER** to a platter and let rest for 10 minutes.

4 **SPREAD** 1 Tbsp (15 mL) of mustard on the bottom half of each bun and 1 Tbsp (15 mL) of aioli on the top half of each bun.

5 **CUT** the pork into thin slices and divide between the buns. Add 1 Tbsp (15 mL) of roasted red peppers, 4 arugula leaves, 1 radicchio leaf, and 3 slices of cheese to each bun. Cover with the top and enjoy!

TONY'S SUGGESTIONS
- **DRY, MEDIUM-BODIED WHITE WINE** *lightly oaked Ontario or BC Chardonnay, white Burgundy, Alsace Pinot Gris*
- **MEDIUM-BODIED RED** *Beaujolais (named villages– Morgon, Fleurie, etc.), red Burgundy, Ontario or BC Pinot Noir*
- **DRY ROSÉ** *Ontario, Tavel*

GURTH'S NOTES
- *Try this with any soft bloomy rind cheese, such as Fleurmier, Ramembert, or Le Noble.*
- *For extra decadence, try a triple crème brie.*
- *Try this with other types of meat, even cold cuts. Thick-sliced grilled vegetables would be delicious, too. Experiment!*
- *Aioli is a French mayonnaise-type condiment. To make your own, stir several cloves of mashed roasted garlic into a store-bought mayonnaise. It also goes great with French fries.*

Grilled Caprese Salad Sandwich

Using Mozzarina Mediterraneo, produced by Saputo Inc. in Saint-Léonard, QC.

I am a master of the grilled cheese sandwich. I began my apprenticeship at a very young age. My formative years saw me starting off with slices of white bread and mozzarella. A few years later I graduated to using wholegrain bread and havarti. Through my culinary education, ethnic breads and other cheese entered my grilled cheese vocabulary. With the growing popularity of panini grills in Canada, I decided to grill the caprese salad, a classic Italian recipe. Has the master gone crazy? Make your decision after you taste this.

2	ciabatta rolls
8	sun-dried tomatoes, soaked in warm water for 15 minutes and sliced
2	Tbsp (30 mL) fresh basil, finely sliced
4	oz (100 g) Mozzarina Mediterraneo, sliced
•	extra virgin olive oil

TONY'S SUGGESTIONS
- **MEDIUM-BODIED, DRY, OLD-WORLD WHITE WINE** *Chablis, Muscadet, Soave, Rueda (Spain)*
- **ACIDIC YOUNG RED WINE** *Barbera, Chianti, Beaujolais*
- **FORTIFIED WINE** *Fino or Manzanilla sherry*
- **BEER** *Pilsner*

GURTH'S NOTES
- *Use a mild cheese such as bocconcini, a mild or medium cheddar, mozzarella, or havarti.*

Cooking Instructions

1 **PREHEAT** the sandwich press, panini grill, or skillet to medium-high.
2 **REMOVE** the top crust of the ciabatta rolls and cut the rolls in half.
3 **PLACE** ½ the sun-dried tomatoes on the bottom of each roll.
4 **DIVIDE** the sliced basil and place over the tomatoes.
5 **DISTRIBUTE** the cheese overtop.
6 **COVER** each roll with the top half.
7 **BRUSH** olive oil on the top of each sandwich.
8 **GRILL** until the top is golden and the cheese has melted.

PREPARATION TIME 30 MINS
COOKING TIME 35 MINS
MAKES 4–6 SERVINGS

La Chute Chaudière Cheddar & Watercress Tart

Using La Chute Chaudière Cheddar, produced by Fromagerie Ferme des Chutes in Saint-Félicien, QC.

People are amazed by the great flavours in this tart and even more surprised when I tell them it contains no eggs. I wish my mother had given me a good slice of this instead of the watercress sandwiches I occasionally found in my lunch bag when I was in high school. The sandwich did not fuel me very well for football practice. But this tart sure would have!

1	Tbsp (15 mL) extra virgin olive oil
1	French shallot, chopped
3	cloves garlic, minced
1	bunch watercress, stems discarded
4	Tbsp (60 mL) plain yogurt
1	+ ½ cups (375 mL) shredded La Chute Chaudière Cheddar
•	pinch of cayenne
2	cups (500 mL) cubed white bread with crust removed
1	9-inch (23-cm) pie shell, store-bought

TONY'S SUGGESTIONS
- **FULL-BODIED, DRY WHITE WINE** *California/Australian Chardonnay, oak-aged Sauvignon Blanc (Fumé Blanc)*
- **MEDIUM-BODIED, DRY RED** *Ontario Cabernet Franc, Cabernet Sauvignon, Syrah*
- **BEER** *Brown ale*

GURTH'S NOTES
- *Try this tart with arugula, spinach, or Swiss chard—or any combination of bitter greens.*
- *Use your favourite local, aged cheddar. Try a raw milk cheddar if it's available.*

Cooking instructions continued on following page . . .

La Chute Chaudière Cheddar & Watercress Tart (continued)
Cooking Instructions

1 **PREHEAT** the oven to 350°F (180°C) and place the oven rack in the centre position.

2 **IN A LARGE SKILLET,** heat the oil over medium-low temperature.

3 **ADD** the shallot and garlic; cook for 2 minutes.

4 **STIR** in the watercress and cook until wilted.

5 **REMOVE** the skillet from the heat. Mix in the yogurt, cheese, and cayenne.

6 **PLACE** the bread cubes in the bottom of the tart shell. Spoon the watercress cheese mixture overtop.

7 **PLACE** the filled shell in the preheated oven and bake for 35 minutes, or until golden brown.

8 **SERVE** immediately.

Beef Tenderloin
with Black Truffle Chèvre & Cranberry Salad

Using Black Truffle Chèvre, produced by Salt Spring Island Cheese Co. on Salt Spring Island, BC.

Where's the vinaigrette or salad dressing? There is none in this recipe. The juices from the beef tenderloin and the melting creamy chèvre give this salad great flavours and just enough moisture.

TONY'S SUGGESTIONS
- **BOLD, OLD-WORLD RED WINE WITH GOOD ACIDITY** *Barolo, Chianti Classico Riserva, Châteauneuf-du-Pape, Crozes-Hermitage, red Bordeaux*
- **FORTIFIED WINE** *10-year-old tawny port*

GURTH'S NOTES
- *Use other creamy, flavoured chèvre.*

3	cups (750 mL) baby romaine, torn
1	stalk celery, peeled and sliced
1	green onion, sliced
½	cup (125 mL) croutons
1	Tbsp (15 mL) extra virgin olive oil
1	lb (500 g) beef tenderloin, thinly sliced
4	+ ½ oz (113 g) Black Truffle Chèvre
⅓	cup (75 mL) dried cranberries
•	kosher salt and freshly ground black pepper, to taste

Cooking Instructions

1 **IN A BOWL,** combine the romaine, celery, green onion, and croutons.

2 **DIVIDE** the salad mixture amongst the plates.

3 **IN A LARGE SKILLET,** heat the oil over medium temperature.

4 **BRIEFLY SEAR** the beef, just to warm it up.

5 **DIVIDE** the tenderloin slices amongst the plates, placing it over the salad.

6 **CRUMBLE** the cheese over the salads and garnish with dried cranberries.

7 **SEASON** with salt and pepper.

Ratatouille Calzones

Using Mozzarina Mediterraneo, produced by Saputo Inc. in Saint-Léonard, QC.

Calzones were quite the rage in restaurants in the 1980s. When I worked my first restaurant job at the Ritz III in Ottawa, we offered several on the menu. One even had chicken as an ingredient, which was considered quite different back then. Many other countries have their own versions of this stuffed dough dish: England's Cornish pasties, Jamaica's patties, Spain's empañadas. Here's my Italian and French twist on it.

2	Tbsp (30 mL) extra virgin olive oil
½	large onion, diced
1	bulb garlic, cloves peeled and halved
½	medium eggplant, cut into ½-inch-thick (1-cm) slices and salted for 60 minutes
1	zucchini, cut into ½-inch (1-cm) dice
1	red bell pepper, cut into ½-inch (1-cm) dice
1	+ ½ cups (375 mL) diced tomatoes
2	bay leaves
3	sprigs fresh thyme
12	black olives, pitted and chopped
2	balls fresh store-bought pizza dough
4	Tbsp (60 mL) finely chopped fresh basil
8	oz (200 g) Mozzarina Mediterraneo, sliced

TONY'S SUGGESTIONS
- **MEDIUM-BODIED, DRY WHITE WINE** *Chardonnay (unoaked), Chablis, Sauvignon Blanc, Soave, Gavi*
- **DRY ROSÉ**
- **RED WINE** *young Zinfandel*
- **BEER** *Brown ale, India Pale Ale*

MAKE AHEAD
- *Ratatouille mixture can be made up to 2 days ahead, covered, and refrigerated.*

GURTH'S NOTES
- *Try this with other mozzarella-style cheeses.*
- *If you are feeling really adventurous, use the ingredients from the Caramelized Onion, Walnut & Bleu de la Moutonnière Pizzenta, page 109. That would make a delicious and different calzone.*

Cooking Instructions

1 **PREHEAT** the oven to 350°F (180°C) and place the oven rack at the centre position. Spray a baking sheet with cooking oil.

2 **IN A LARGE SAUCEPAN,** heat the olive oil over medium temperature. Stir in the onion, cover, and cook for 5 to 7 minutes, or until softened.

3 **STIR** in the garlic and cook for 2 minutes.

4 **RINSE** the eggplant and pat dry with paper towels. Cut into cubes.

5 **ADD** the eggplant, zucchini, red pepper, tomatoes, bay leaves, and thyme sprigs to the saucepan. Bring to a boil. Reduce the heat to a simmer and cook for approximately 30 minutes.

6 **ADD** the olives and cook for another 5 minutes.

7 **LIGHTLY** dust a work surface with flour. Roll 1 of the balls of dough into a large circle ¼ inch (6 mm) thick.

8 **PLACE** ½ of the vegetable mixture, 2 Tbsp (30-mL) of the basil, and ½ of the cheese slices on half of the circle.

9 **FOLD** the dough over to form a semi-circle. Press the edges to seal. Place on the prepared baking sheet.

10 **REPEAT** steps 7 to 9 with the remaining ingredients.

11 **BAKE** in the preheated oven for 20 to 25 minutes, or until the crust is golden.

12 **REMOVE** the calzones, cut into wedges, and serve immediately.

Quark & Fundy Smoked Salmon Gâteau

Using Plain Quark, produced by Armadale Farms in Roachdale, NB.

I modified this recipe from one I learned from Chef Stephen Langley, one of my professors at George Brown College's Chef School. I have served it at many different catered functions as an appetizer, for brunch, or as lunch main course.

2	eggs, lightly beaten
1	cup (250 mL) milk
½	cup (125 mL) water
3	Tbsp (45 mL) melted unsalted butter, cooled
½	tsp (2 mL) kosher salt
1	cup (250 mL) all-purpose flour
1	cup (250 mL) Plain Quark
1	medium red onion, finely diced
3	Tbsp (45 mL) finely chopped fresh dill
27	oz (675 g) Atlantic smoked salmon, sliced
•	fresh dill springs, for garnish

Cooking instructions continued on following page . . .

TONY'S SUGGESTIONS
- **VERY DRY WHITE WINE** *Alsace or German Riesling, dry Ontario Riesling, dry Gewurztraminer, Sauvignon Blanc from the Loire, unoaked Ontario or BC Chardonnay*
- **BEER** *Pilsner, smoked beer*
- **SPIRITS** *Ice-cold vodka, single malt whisky*

MAKE AHEAD
- *Crêpes can be made a week ahead and refrigerated; place waxed paper between each crêpe and cover the stack in plastic wrap. Crêpes can also be frozen.*
- *The batter can be made a day ahead, covered, and refrigerated.*
- *The gâteau recipe can be made a day ahead, covered, and refrigerated.*

GURTH'S NOTES
- *If quark is unavailable, use cream cheese.*
- *You will produce more crêpes than required for 1 gâteau. Freeze the rest for future use.*

Quark & Fundy Smoked Salmon Gâteau (continued)
Cooking Instructions

1   **IN A SMALL BOWL,** combine the eggs, milk, water, and butter.

2   **IN A LARGE BOWL,** mix the salt and flour. Pour in the egg mixture, stir until well blended, cover, and refrigerate for an hour.

3   **STRAIN** the batter into a clean bowl to remove any lumps.

4   **HEAT** a medium skillet to medium-high and brush with a little butter. Pour in 3 Tbsp (45 mL) of the batter and tilt the pan, allowing the crêpe batter to cover the entire surface of the skillet.

5   **COOK** until lightly golden along the edges; flip and cook for 30 seconds.

6   **TRANSFER** the crêpe to a plate and allow to cool before covering with waxed paper.

7   **REPEAT** with the remaining batter.

8   **PLACE** 1 crêpe on a large plate or platter. Spread a small amount of quark on it, and sprinkle with the diced red onions and chopped dill.

9   **COVER** with 3 to 4 slices of smoked salmon. Place a second crêpe on top.

10   **REPEAT** until all the cheese, onions, dill, and salmon are used.

11   **COVER** and refrigerate for 60 minutes.

12   **SLICE** into pie-shaped pieces and garnish each serving with a sprig of dill.

PREPARATION TIME 30 MINS
+ 1 HR REFRIGERATION
COOKING TIME 10 MINS
MAKES 4 SERVINGS

Greek Lamb Feta Pita

Using Feta produced by Skotidakis Goat Farm in St. Eugène, ON.

Joanne and I love eating locally raised lamb. It is tender, juicy, and not too gamey. We buy it from our neighbourhood butcher who butterflies the leg for us.

4	cloves garlic, minced
2	shallots, finely diced
6	Tbsp (90 mL) extra virgin olive oil
1	lb (500 g) butterflied leg of lamb
7	oz (175 g) feta, cubed
1	cucumber, peeled, seeded, and diced
1	bulb fennel, shaved into thin strips
1	Tbsp (15 mL) dried mint
3	Tbsp (45 mL) freshly squeezed lemon juice
4	pitas, halved

Cooking Instructions

1   **IN A SMALL BOWL,** combine the garlic, shallots, and 4 Tbsp (60 mL) of the olive oil.

2   **PLACE** the lamb in a non-metallic container, and pour the mixture overtop. Cover and refrigerate for 1 hour.

3   **IN A SECOND** non-metallic bowl, combine the feta, cucumber, fennel, remaining 2 Tbsp (30 mL) olive oil, mint, and lemon juice. Set aside.

4   **PLACE** a large skillet over medium-high heat. Pour a little bit of the lamb marinade into the pan.

5   **COOK** the lamb for 5 minutes on each side. Transfer to a plate and cover with foil for 10 minutes.

6   **CUT** the lamb into thin slices. Spoon part of the fennel/cucumber mixture into the pita. Add a few slices of lamb and top with more fennel mixture

7   **SERVE** immediately.

TONY'S SUGGESTIONS
- **MEDIUM-BODIED, DRY RED WINE** *Cabernet Sauvignon from Chile, Australia's Barossa Valley or Ontario or BC Pinot Noir, Aglianico (Greece), Beaujolais-Villages*
- **BEER** *Brown ale*

MAKE AHEAD
- *Lamb can be marinated 1 day ahead, covered, and refrigerated. Fennel/cucumber mixture can be made 1 day ahead, covered, and refrigerated.*

GURTH'S NOTES
- *Serve these pitas with tzatziki sauce.*
- *Substitute chicken, turkey, or pork for the lamb.*
- *Try this with Duro Blanco cheese.*
- *Try rolling it in a wrap for a tasty lunch.*
- *This is a great way to use any leftover lamb, whether it's a leg, shoulder, or chop.*

Turkey Mamirolle Melt

Using Le Mamirolle, produced by Fromagerie Éco-Délices Inc. in Plessisville, QC.

Enjoy this delicious sandwich using leftovers, purchase a turkey breast and cook it, or buy prepared sliced turkey. There's no need to limit this sandwich to Thanksgiving and Christmas!

4	Tbsp (60 mL) cranberry jelly
1	large sourdough loaf, top removed, and centre gouged out
2	lb (1 kg) turkey breast, cooked and sliced
1	cup (250 mL) arugula
6	oz (150 g) Le Mamirolle, sliced

Cooking Instructions

1 **PREHEAT** the oven to 350°F (180°C) and place the oven rack in the centre position.
2 **SPOON** the cranberry jelly on the inside bottom of the bread.
3 **PLACE** the turkey, arugula, and cheese in the cavity.
4 **REPLACE** the top and wrap the entire loaf in foil.
5 **PLACE** on a baking sheet and bake in the preheated oven for 20 to 25 minutes.
6 **UNWRAP** and cut the sandwich into triangles.

TONY'S SUGGESTIONS
- **LIGHT RED WINE** *Beaujolais, unoaked Argentinean Malbec, red Burgundy, Ontario/BC Pinot Noir*
- **MEDIUM-BODIED FRUITY WHITE WINE** *fruity Zinfandel*

GURTH'S NOTES
- *Many types of cheese can work in this sandwich. Use your favourite, or whatever happens to be in your fridge!*
- *Use leftovers—this sandwich is particularly handy after Thanksgiving or Christmas.*

Warm Chicken Salad Sandwich
with Ciel de Charlevoix

Using Ciel de Charlevoix, produced by La Maison d'affinage Maurice Dufour Inc. in Baie-Saint-Paul, QC.

Here's a delicious twist on the classic chicken salad sandwich.

1	cup (250 mL) chopped cooked chicken
1	stalk celery, peeled and diced
½	small red onion, finely diced
3	oz (75 g) Ciel de Charlevoix, crumbled
2	large croissants

Cooking Instructions

1   **IN A BOWL,** combine the chicken, celery, and onions.

2   **IN A SMALL SAUCEPAN,** melt the cheese over medium-low heat.

3   **STIR** the melted cheese into the chicken mixture.

4   **CUT** the croissants in half. Divide the filling between them and replace the tops. Serve immediately.

TONY'S SUGGESTIONS
- **MEDIUM-BODIED, DRY WHITE WINE** *Viognier, California Chardonnay, New Zealand Sauvignon Blanc*
- **RED WINE** *Argentinean Malbec, Chilean Carmenère*
- **ROSÉ** *Tavel*
- **BEER** *Belgian ale, India Pale Ale*

MAKE AHEAD
- *Use leftover chicken.*

GURTH'S NOTES
- *This sandwich can be made with leftover roast beef, turkey, or pork. A vegetarian sandwich would be good, too.*
- *Use other blue cheese, such as Borgonzola, Ermite bleu, Dragon's Breath, Beddis Blue, or Stilton.*

CLOCKWISE FROM TOP-RIGHT Black Peppercorn-Rubbed Rib-Eye Canapés with Smoked Gouda, *page 66;* Mini Smoked Turkey Pizzas with Green Peppers, Red Onions, Roasted Garlic & Colby, *page 74;* Savoury Cheddar Bacon Truffles, *page 72;* Smoked Trout, Roasted Red Pepper & Fou du Roy Mini-Quiche, *page 73.*

HORS D'OEUVRE

Black Peppercorn-Rubbed Rib-Eye Canapés
with Smoked Gouda *(pictured on page 64)*

Using Smoked Gouda, produced by Gort's Gouda Cheese Farm in Salmon Arm, BC.

Here is a tasty canapé that will keep all the carnivores at your next party happy. They may circle around the table like vultures once the platter is empty, hoping more will appear for them to devour.

3	Tbsp (45 mL) cracked black peppercorns
2	rib-eye steaks (6 oz/150 g each)
1	Tbsp (15 mL) unsalted butter
1	Tbsp (15 mL) extra virgin olive oil
½	white onion, thinly sliced
20	slices fresh baguette
20	slices Smoked Gouda
•	fresh parsley, for garnish

TONY'S SUGGESTIONS
- **FULL-BODIED, DRY RED WINE** *Zinfandel, Châteauneuf-du-Pape, Amarone, Primitivo*
- **BEER** *Porter*

MAKE AHEAD
- *Steak and onions can be cooked a day ahead, covered, and refrigerated.*

GURTH'S NOTES
- *You can substitute a flavoured Gouda, Monterey Jack, havarti, or double-smoked cheddar for the Smoked Gouda.*

Cooking Instructions

1 **RUB** the peppercorns onto all the surfaces of the steaks.

2 **HEAT** a large skillet to medium-high and melt the butter.

3 **COOK** the steaks for 4 to 5 minutes on each side, to medium-rare. Transfer the steaks to a plate, cover with foil, and let rest for 10 minutes.

4 **USING THE SAME SKILLET,** warm the oil over medium-low heat. Add the sliced onions, cover, and cook for 5 minutes, or until translucent.

5 **CUT** the steaks against the grain into long thin slices.

6 **DISTRIBUTE** the steak evenly over the baguette slices and top with the cooked onions, then a slice of cheese.

7 **PLACE** the canapés on a baking sheet.

8 **PREHEAT** the broiler and place the oven rack at the second-highest level.

9 **BROIL** the canapés until the cheese has melted, about 30 to 60 seconds.

10 **COOL** briefly, garnish with a parsley leaf, and serve.

PREPARATION TIME 20 MINS

COOKING TIME 0 MINS

MAKES 4 SERVINGS

The Nurnberg Canapé

Using Le Noble cheese, produced by Fromagerie Domaine Féodal in Berthierville, QC.

In 2006, I worked as the Canadian Chef at our nation's pavilion at Biofach, an international organic food trade show in Nurnberg, Germany. For one of the cocktail receptions, the on-site caterer provided a tray of canapés with ham and cheese, garnished with grapes. I sampled one and was surprised how delicious this simple hors d'oeuvre was. I pass on to you my version of that Nurnberg discovery.

1	baguette
6	slices Westphalian ham
12	slices Le Noble cheese
18	seedless green grapes, halved

Cooking Instructions

1 **CUT** the baguette on a diagonal into 12 slices.

2 **CUT** the ham to cover each slice of bread.

3 **COVER** with a slice of cheese.

4 **GARNISH** with 3 grape halves.

TONY'S SUGGESTIONS

- **LIGHT RED WINE**
  Beaujolais, Ontario or BC Gamay or Pinot Noir
- **DRY ROSÉ** *Tavel or Bandol*
- **AROMATIC WHITE WINE**
  Off-dry Riesling
- **BEER** *Pale ale*

MAKE AHEAD

- *Make the canapés 90 minutes before planning to serve them. This permits the flavours and aroma of the cheese to awaken fully.*

GURTH'S NOTES

- *Use other soft bloomy rind cheese, such as brie, Camembert, Triple Crème, Island Bries, or St-Clair.*

PREPARATION TIME 40 MINS
COOKING TIME O MINS
MAKES 10 SERVINGS

Spanish Fresh Cheese Appetizer

Using Queso Fresco Cheese, produced by Portuguese Cheese Co. in Toronto, ON.

*George DeMelo, co-owner and cheesemaker at Portuguese Cheese Co.,
gave me this recipe when I visited his facility. So few Torontonians
know about his company, which is one of just two cheesemaking
establishments within this city of 2.5 million. It's one of Toronto's
secret jewels.*

½	lb (250 g) Queso Fresco Cheese
3	cloves garlic, minced
1	tsp (5 mL) dried oregano
•	pinch freshly ground black pepper
3	Tbsp (45 mL) extra virgin olive oil
•	crackers or crusty bread

TONY'S SUGGESTIONS
- **MEDIUM-BODIED, DRY WHITE WINE** *Rueda, Orvieto, Greco di Tufo, Pinot Grigio*
- **RED** *Chianti, Sangiovese, Ontario or BC Gamay*
- **BEER** *Wheat beer*

MAKE AHEAD
- *Make the day before, cover, and refrigerate.*

GURTH'S NOTES
- *Fresh mozzarella, cheddar, or boccocini are possible substitutes.*

Cooking Instructions

1 **USING A CHEESE GRATER,** shred the cheese into a bowl.

2 **PLACE** the garlic in a medium bowl. Add the oregano, pepper, and 1 Tbsp (15 mL) of the oil. Mix thoroughly.

3 **ADD** the cheese and toss.

4 **ADD** the remaining oil and toss lightly.

5 **COVER** the mixture and let sit at room temperature for 30 minutes to allow the flavours to blend. Mix lightly before serving.

6 **TO SERVE,** spoon the mixture onto hard wheat crackers or crusty bread.

Queso Picante with Mushrooms

Using Monterey Jack, produced by Ivanhoe Cheese Inc. in Ivanhoe, ON.

I remember eating a version of this dish when I was 13, visiting family friends in Mexico City. It was a crowd pleaser then and my re-creation was very popular with both Joanne and Shannon, our assistant.

1	Tbsp (15 mL) extra virgin olive oil
1	dried chipotle chili, soaked in warm water
3	cloves garlic, minced
4	oz (100 g) cremini mushrooms, coarsely chopped
•	kosher salt and freshly ground black pepper, to taste
12	oz (300 g) Monterey Jack, shredded
1	green onion, thinly sliced
2	tsp (10 mL) finely chopped jalapeño chili
•	tortilla chips, for dipping

TONY'S SUGGESTIONS
- SWEETISH WHITE WINE WITH GOOD ACIDITY
  semi-dry Vouvray, Viognier, Riesling Spätlese, Ontario Late Harvest Riesling
- SPARKLING WINE
  Asti Spumante

GURTH'S NOTES
- *Try other types of dried chilis in this dish. For more heat, use a jalapeño or chili-flavoured cheese.*

Cooking Instructions

1 **IN A MEDIUM SKILLET,** heat the oil over low temperature.

2 **ADD** the chipotle chili and garlic; cook for 2 minutes.

3 **INCREASE** the heat to medium, add the mushrooms, and cook for another 5 minutes. Season with salt and pepper.

4 **STIR** in the cheese and cook until it begins to bubble.

5 **GARNISH** with the green onion and jalapeño.

6 **SERVE** right out of the skillet with the tortilla chips on the side.

PREPARATION TIME 20 MINS
  + 3 HRS REFRIGERATION
COOKING TIME 10 MINS
MAKES 24 PIECES

Savoury Cheddar Bacon Truffles

(pictured on page 64)

Using Village Cheddar, produced by The Village Cheese Co. in Armstrong, BC.

This recipe comes from the files of the Village Cheese Co. Joanne tested it and gave the recipe two thumbs up.

6	slices side bacon, chopped
8	oz (200 g) Old or Extra Old Village 3-year-old Cheddar, cubed
¼	cup (60 mL) unsalted butter, cubed
2	Tbsp (30 mL) chopped parsley
2	Tbsp (30 mL) sliced green onions
2	Tbsp (30 mL) store-bought, drained hot banana pepper rings
¾	cup (175 mL) pecans, toasted and finely chopped

Cooking Instructions

1 **COOK** the bacon until crisp. Drain well, reserving 1 Tbsp (15 mL) of the drippings. Set the bacon and drippings aside.

2 **COMBINE** the cheese, butter, parsley, green onions, and pepper rings in a food processor. Process until smooth, stopping the machine to scrape down the sides of the bowl with a rubber spatula as necessary.

3 **ADD** the bacon and the drippings to the mixture and process until the bacon is finely chopped.

4 **CHILL** the mixture for about 3 hours, or until firm enough to roll. Form into 2 dozen truffles, about 1-inch (2.5-cm) in diameter.

5 **ROLL** the truffles in the chopped pecans.

TONY'S SUGGESTIONS
- **SPICY, AROMATIC WHITE WINE WITH SOME SWEETNESS** *Ontario Semi-Dry Riesling, German Riesling Spätlese, Viognier, Alsace Pinot Gris, white Zinfandel*
- **FORTIFIED WINE** *Dry Oloroso sherry*
- **BEER** *Brown ale*

MAKE AHEAD
- *Truffles can be made up to 2 days prior to serving, covered, and refrigerated.*

GURTH'S NOTES
- *For other tasty recipes from The Village Cheese Co., visit their website, www.villagecheese.com.*

PREPARATION TIME 20 MINS
COOKING TIME 15 MINS
MAKES 10 PIECES

Smoked Trout, Roasted Red Pepper
& Fou du Roy Mini-Quiche *(pictured on page 64)*

Using Fou du Roy, produced by Les Fromagiers de la Table Ronde in Sainte-Sophie, QC.

In these wonderful mini-quiches, the sweetness of the roasted peppers and smokiness of the trout are bound together by the creaminess of the cheese.

2	eggs, lightly beaten
¼	cup (60 mL) milk
2	Tbsp (30 mL) diced roasted red bell pepper
3	Tbsp (45 mL) finely diced Fou du Roy cheese
2	Tbsp (30 mL) finely sliced smoked trout
10	store-bought tart shells, pre-baked following manufacturer's directions

Cooking Instructions

1 **PREHEAT** the oven to 350°F (180°C) and place the oven rack in the middle position.

2 **IN A SMALL BOWL,** combine the eggs, milk, red pepper, cheese, and trout.

3 **DIVIDE** the mixture evenly amongst the tart shells. Place them on a baking sheet.

4 **BAKE** in the preheated oven for 10 to 15 minutes, or until the filling is set.

5 **REMOVE** from the oven and let cool for 5 to 10 minutes before serving.

TONY'S SUGGESTIONS
- **CRISP, DRY WHITE WINE**
Sauvignon Blanc from the Loire or Ontario, Chablis, Muscadet, Aligoté

MAKE AHEAD
- Mini-quiches can be baked a day ahead, covered, and refrigerated. Reheat in a 300°F (150°C) oven for 10 minutes.

GURTH'S NOTES
- Use your favourite semi-soft, washed rind cheese, such as Oka, Le Baluchon, Migneron de Charlevoix, Mamirolle, or a soft, bloomy rind cheese like brie, Savoury Moon, or goat brie.
- Smoked sturgeon, scallops, oysters, eel, whitefish, or arctic char would be a tasty substitute for the trout.

Mini Smoked Turkey Pizzas
with Green Peppers, Red Onions, Roasted Garlic & Colby *(pictured on page 64)*

Using Colby, produced by Saint-Albert Cheese Co-operative in Saint-Albert, ON.

Who doesn't like pizza? These little treats will disappear as soon as you put the tray on the coffee table—if they survive the trip from the kitchen.

2	Tbsp (30 mL) extra virgin olive oil
1	medium red onion, thinly sliced
1	green bell pepper, seeded and thinly sliced
4	oz (100 g) sliced smoked turkey breast
1	small can of pizza sauce (4 oz/114 mL)
1	large prebaked pizza crust
2	bulbs garlic, cloves roasted and peeled
6	oz (150 g) Colby cheese, crumbled

TONY'S SUGGESTIONS
- **YOUTHFUL, ACIDIC RED WINE** *Barbera, Chianti, Valpolicella, Ontario Gamay*
- **BEER** *Lager, Pilsner, amber ale*

MAKE AHEAD
- *Garlic can be roasted and peeled 2 days ahead of time, covered, and refrigerated. Peppers and onions can be cooked 2 hours ahead of time, covered, and refrigerated.*

GURTH'S NOTES
- *Use your favourite sliced deli meat, such as Cajun chicken, ham, or salami.*
- *Use another melting cheese, like havarti, Edam, or provolone.*

Cooking Instructions

1 **PREHEAT** the oven to 375°F (190°C) and place the oven rack in the centre position. Grease a baking sheet.

2 **IN A LARGE SKILLET** over medium-low temperature, heat 1 Tbsp (15 mL) of the oil. Add the onion and cook, covered, for 4 to 5 minutes, or until softened.

3 **TRANSFER** the onion to a bowl and set aside.

4 **IN THE SAME SKILLET,** heat the remaining 1 Tbsp (15 mL) of oil over medium temperature and cook the green pepper for 4 minutes, or until tender.

5 **ROLL** up 5 slices of turkey breast, and cut into thin slices across the roll. Repeat with the remaining slices.

6 **SPOON** the pizza sauce over the pizza crust.

7 **ARRANGE** the sliced turkey meat, onions, green pepper, and whole cloves of roasted garlic over the sauce.

8 **SCATTER** the cheese overtop.

9 **PLACE** on the prepared baking sheet and bake for 10 to 15 minutes, or until the cheese has melted.

10 **REMOVE** from the oven and let cool briefly. Cut into bite-sized squares.

Chili Pepperonato-Stuffed Risotto Balls

Using Pepperonato, produced by Salerno Dairy in Hamilton, ON.

Joanne and I made a variation of this recipe several years ago, following the traditional way of deep-frying the balls. They were a great hit at the party but what were we to do with the leftover oil? We don't deep-fry food often. This is our pan-fried and baked version—as tasty as the original and also healthier. See if you can identify the Canadian twist on this classic Italian recipe.

2	cups (500 mL) risotto, cooked following manufacturer's directions, cooled
2	large eggs, lightly beaten
1 + ⅓	cups (325 mL) breadcrumbs
4	tsp (20 mL) dried basil
⅓	cup (75 mL) Red River cereal
3	oz (75 g) Pepperonato, cut into ½-inch (1–cm) cubes
3	Tbsp (45 mL) canola oil
•	kosher salt and freshly ground black pepper, to taste
2	cups (500 mL) store-bought, roasted red pepper tomato sauce, heated

TONY'S SUGGESTIONS
- **POWERFUL RED WINE WITH SOME SWEETNESS** *Amarone, Primitivo, Zinfandel, Argentinean Malbec*
- **BEER** *Lager, Pilsner*

MAKE AHEAD
- *Risotto can be cooked a day ahead, covered, and refrigerated.*

GURTH'S NOTES
- *If Pepperonato is not available, use Monterey Jack, havarti, or mozzarella.*

Cooking Instructions

1 **IN A LARGE BOWL,** combine the risotto, eggs, and 1 cup (250 mL) of the breadcrumbs.

2 **IN A MEDIUM BOWL,** combine the remaining ⅓ cup (75 mL) breadcrumbs with the basil and Red River cereal.

3 **PLACE** a heaping tablespoon (15 mL) of the risotto mixture in the palm of your hand.

4 **INSERT** a cube of Pepperonato into the centre and form into a ball, completely enclosing the cheese.

5 **ROLL** the ball in the breadcrumb mixture.

6 **REPEAT** with the remaining risotto mixture and cheese cubes.

7 **PREHEAT** the oven to 350°F (180°C) and place the oven rack in the centre position.

8 **PLACE** a large, heavy skillet over medium heat and add the oil.

9 **WHEN THE OIL IS HOT,** fry the rice balls in small batches, turning them frequently and cooking until they're golden.

10 **TRANSFER** the balls to a baking sheet and bake for 5 minutes.

11 **SEASON** with salt and pepper. Let rest for 2 minutes.

12 **SERVE** hot with the heated tomato sauce for dipping.

Stuffed Baby Potatoes
with Horseradish Cheddar

Using Horseradish Cheddar, produced by Ivanhoe Cheese Inc. in Ivanhoe, ON.

This recipe was inspired by hors d'oeuvre my mother served several years ago at a Christmas cocktail party. Thank you for the idea, Mom.

12	baby potatoes
3	oz (75 g) Horseradish Cheddar, shredded
1	tsp (5 mL) dried savory
•	kosher salt and freshly ground black pepper, to taste

Cooking Instructions

1 **PLACE** the potatoes in a medium saucepan and add enough cold water to cover. Cook over high heat until the potatoes are just tender when probed with the tip of a knife. Drain and place in cold water until cool enough to handle.

2 **REMOVE** the top of each potato and set it aside.

3 **USING A MELON BALLER,** scoop out the centre of each potato and place in a bowl.

4 **MASH** the potato flesh. Combine with the cheese and savory. Season with salt and pepper.

5 **USING A PASTRY BAG WITH A STAR TIP,** pipe the mixture back into the potato shell and replace the top. Serve at room temperature.

TONY'S SUGGESTIONS
- **BOLD RED WINE** *California Zinfandel or Chilean Cabernet Sauvignon; Oregon Pinot or New Zealand Pinot Noir*
- **BEER** *Brown ale, India Pale Ale*

MAKE AHEAD
- *Stuffed potatoes can be made a day ahead, covered, and refrigerated. Bring to room temperature 60 minutes prior to serving.*

GURTH'S NOTES
- *Use other flavoured cheese, such as cheddar, havarti, Gouda, or Monterey Jack.*

Gouda & Mushroom Wrap

**Using Caraway Gouda, produced by Armadale Farms in Roachville, NB;
and plain Quark, produced by Fox Hill Cheese House in Port Williams, NS.**

*Served either as an hors d'oeuvre, or cut in half as a warm sandwich for
lunch, this is an easy and tasty treat.*

1	Tbsp (15 mL) extra virgin olive oil
2	shallots, finely diced
2	cloves garlic, minced
10	white mushrooms, stems removed and caps diced
2	Tbsp (30 mL) plain quark
2	large (10-inch/25-cm) flour tortillas
3	oz (75 g) Caraway Gouda, shredded
4	Boston lettuce leaves

Cooking Instructions

1   **IN A MEDIUM-SIZED SKILLET,** heat the oil over medium-low temperature.
    Add the shallots and garlic and cook for 2 minutes.

2   **STIR** in the mushrooms, and cook for 7 to 10 minutes.

3   **REMOVE** the skillet from the heat and let the mixture cool.

4   **SPREAD** 1 Tbsp (15 mL) of the quark on each tortilla. Sprinkle with
    the shredded Gouda. Place the lettuce leaves over the cheese.

5   **SPOON** the mushroom mixture across the centre. Roll the
    tortillas tightly.

6   **ENCLOSE** tightly in plastic wrap and refrigerate for 60 minutes.

7   **PREHEAT** the oven to 350°F (180°C).

8   **REMOVE** the plastic from the tortilla wraps and wrap in foil; place in the
    preheated oven for 5 to 10 minutes.

9   **REMOVE** from the oven and cool momentarily before unwrapping. Slice
    into 1-inch (2.5-cm) rounds and serve.

TONY'S SUGGESTIONS
- **AROMATIC WHITE WINE**
  *Gewurztraminer, Riesling
  Kabinett, Viognier*
- **FORTIFIED WINE**
  Fino sherry
- **BEER**
  Belgian Saison, porter

MAKE AHEAD
- *Tortilla wraps can be assembled
  1 day ahead, wrapped, and
  refrigerated. Bake just before
  serving.*

GURTH'S NOTES
- *Instead of quark, use cream
  cheese.*
- *Instead of Gouda, use your
  favourite flavoured cheese*
- *A jalapeño Gouda or pepper
  Monterey Jack would be very
  tasty here.*

Vintage Puff Straws

Using Vintage, produced by Carmelis Goat Cheese Artisan in Kelowna, BC.

Carmelis's Vintage cheese is a unique hard goat cheese soaked in red wine for several days, giving it a deep burgundy-coloured rind. I first learned the original recipe for this snack when I worked in the pastry kitchen at Toronto's North 44 restaurant. They were popular with patrons of the upstairs lounge, especially with a glass of good wine.

2	tsp (10 mL) all-purpose flour
1	10- × 10-inch (25- × 25-cm) sheet puff pastry
1	egg, beaten with 1 tsp (5 mL) water, at room temperature
1	tsp (5 mL) herbes de Provence
½	oz (12 g) Vintage cheese, grated

Cooking Instructions

1 **PREHEAT** the oven to 425°F (220°C) and place the oven rack in the middle position. Line a baking sheet with parchment paper.

2 **LIGHTLY DUST** your work surface with the flour and unroll the pastry.

3 **BRUSH** the dough with the beaten egg.

4 **SPRINKLE** the herbes de Provence over the dough.

5 **SPRINKLE** the cheese overtop, lightly pressing it into the dough.

6 **CUT** the pastry sheet into 16 equal lengths with a pastry cutter.

7 **WORKING WITH 1 STRIP AT A TIME,** twist it several times and place on the prepared baking sheet.

8 **BAKE** in the oven for 7 minutes, or until golden.

TONY'S SUGGESTIONS
- **DRY, MEDIUM-BODIED WHITE WINE**
  Sauvignon Blanc from New Zealand or Ontario, unoaked Chardonnay
- **SPARKLING WINE**
  Champagne or Blanc de blancs
- **BEER**
  Pale ale

MAKE AHEAD
- *Puff straws can be made a day ahead, covered, and kept at room temperature.*

GURTH'S NOTES
- *Substitute a strong-flavoured hard cheese, such as Asiago, Tomme de champ doré, Romano, or Parmesan.*

Kinder Spanakopita

Using Munster, produced by Ivanhoe Cheese Inc. in Ivanhoe, ON.

I remember to this day the first time my mother made the classic Greek spanakopita filled with spinach and feta; it was for a dinner party when we lived in Ottawa. They were tasty but not very kid-friendly. The feta was too salty for my young taste buds. I suggested she should use Munster instead. So here is my kinder version for the kinderfolk.

1	10-oz (250-g) bag baby spinach
2	cups (500 mL) shredded Munster
•	kosher salt and freshly ground black pepper, to taste
12	sheets phyllo pastry
⅔	cup (150 mL) unsalted butter, melted

TONY'S SUGGESTIONS
- **AROMATIC WHITE WINE**
  Alsace Gewurztraminer or Muscat, Riesling
- **RED WINE**
  Beaujolais
- **FORTIFIED WINE**
  Fino or Oloroso sherry
- **BEER**
  Belgian, brown ale

MAKE AHEAD
- *These can be made to the baking stage and frozen. Place on a baking sheet lined with waxed paper and freeze. Transfer to a container or freezer bag when frozen.*
* *Do not thaw before baking. To bake frozen triangles, set the oven at 375°F (190°C); otherwise they brown too much before cooking the filling.*

GURTH'S NOTES
- *Use any good melting cheese (mozzarella, havarti, Edam, Esrom).*
- *Combine with any other cooked vegetables. A tasty way to get your 5 to 10 servings of veggies a day!*

Cooking Instructions

1 **PREHEAT** the oven to 400°F (200°C) and place the rack in the centre position.

2 **IN A SAUCEPAN** with 1 Tbsp (15 mL) of water, cook the spinach over medium-low heat until wilted, approximately 4 minutes. Drain the spinach and let cool. When it's cool enough to handle, squeeze out the excess moisture. Chop and place in a bowl.

3 **COMBINE** the cheese and spinach, mixing well. Add a dash of salt and pepper.

4 **REMOVE** the phyllo from the package, unroll, and cover with a clean, dry tea towel.

5 **PLACE** 1 phyllo sheet on a clean work surface with the short side facing you, and brush lightly with the melted butter.

6 **STACK** a second sheet of phyllo on the first; brush with butter. Repeat with a third sheet.

7 **CUT** the stack lengthwise into 4 strips.

8 **PLACE** 2 Tbsp (30 mL) of the Munster/spinach mixture near the bottom of each strip.

9 **FOLD** the bottom right corner of 1 strip up and over the filling, forming a triangular shape at the bottom. Press down on the top edge. Fold the point of the triangle upwards. Press down along the long edge. Fold the bottom left-hand corner up and over to the opposite side of the strip, creating a triangular shape again, with the filling in the centre. Continue rolling up and over until you reach the top of the strip.

10 **PRESS** down on the top edge.

11 **BRUSH** with more melted butter, and fold the seam over.

12 **PLACE** on a baking sheet and brush the top surface with melted butter. Repeat with the remaining 3 strips of phyllo.

13 **REPEAT** with the remaining sheets of phyllo.

14 **BAKE** in the preheated oven for approximately 7 to 10 minutes, or until golden.

PREPARATION TIME 10 MINS
COOKING TIME 15 MINS
MAKES 3 CUPS (750 ML)

Warm Artichoke & Cheddar Dip

Using Extra Old Cheddar, produced by Laiterie Chalifoux Inc./Fromages Riviera in Sorel-Tracy, QC.

I first prepared this dip when I worked at Château Élan Resort and Winery in Braselton, Georgia, during the 1996 Atlanta Olympics. On occasion, I was asked to prepare this for the patrons of our upstairs lounge. They enjoyed snacking on it after a round of golf or tennis. The day after I prepared a gallon of the dip for the lounge, their cook came to see me, asking where it was. I was perplexed. It had been properly stored in a container, covered, dated, and labelled when I placed it in the walk-in fridge the night before. I discovered later that the banquet chef, one of my superiors, went on a cleaning binge in the fridge earlier that day. He used the dip I made for that day's lunch special for the staff cafeteria. C'est la vie!

TONY'S SUGGESTIONS
- **MEDIUM-BODIED DRY WHITE WINE**
  Sauvignon Blanc from the Loire or Ontario, Grüner Veltliner, Alsace Pinot Gris, Italian Pinot Grigio
- **FORTIFIED WINE**
  Manzanilla sherry (chilled)

MAKE AHEAD
- *Dip can be made 2 days ahead, covered, and refrigerated. Reheat in a saucepan over medium-low temperature or in a microwave oven.*

GURTH'S NOTES
- *Medium to old cheddar, havarti, Edam, or Gouda can be used instead.*

2	Tbsp (30 mL) unsalted butter
2	Tbsp (30 mL) all-purpose flour
1	cup (250 mL) milk
2	oz (50 g) Extra Old Cheddar, shredded
1	can (14 oz/398 mL) artichoke hearts, drained and coarsely chopped
•	dash of hot sauce
•	corn tortilla chips or peeled vegetables, for dipping

Cooking Instructions

1. **IN A MEDIUM SAUCEPAN** over medium-low heat, melt the butter.
2. **STIR** in the flour and cook for 3 minutes.
3. **SLOWLY POUR** the milk into the mixture, whisking constantly. Cook for 5 to 7 minutes, until thick, stirring occasionally.
4. **STIR** in the cheese and artichokes, and season with the hot sauce.
5. **POUR** into a bowl and enjoy while still warm, scooping it up with the tortilla chips or fresh vegetables.

Mini Gouda Gougères

Using Caraway Gouda, produced by Armadale Farms Ltd. in Roachville, NB.

WARNING! *These tasty and light treats are addictive. While nibbling on the first one, your hand automatically is reaching for a second.*

1	cup (250 mL)	water
½	cup (125 mL)	unsalted butter
½	tsp (2 mL)	kosher salt
1	cup (250 mL)	all-purpose flour
4	oz (100 g)	Caraway Gouda, shredded
3		eggs

TONY'S SUGGESTIONS

- **MEDIUM-BODIED WHITE WINE**
  White Burgundy, unoaked Chardonnay
- **FRUITY RED WINE**
  chilled Beaujolais, Ontario Pinot Noir
- **DRY SPARKLING WHITE WINE**
  Champagne or Crémant de Bourgogne
- **BEER**
  Brown ale

MAKE AHEAD

- *Gougères can be made a day ahead, covered, and kept at room temperature. Freeze them for up to a month.*

GURTH'S NOTES

- *Canadian Gouda comes in many different flavours: dill, cumin, smoked, cloves, jalapeño, garlic, red chili pepper, fine herbs, pepper and mustard, fenugreek, nettle—have fun and experiment with these.*

Cooking Instructions

1   **PREHEAT** the oven to 425°F (220°C) and place the oven rack in the middle position.

2   **IN A SMALL SAUCEPAN,** bring the water and butter to a boil.

3   **REMOVE** the pan from the heat and stir in the salt and flour.

4   **COOK** the flour mixture for 30 seconds on the stove, stirring constantly.

5   **STIR** in the cheese.

6   **CRACK** 1 egg into the mixture and stir well until the egg is incorporated. Add the remaining eggs 1 at a time, stirring well after each addition.

7   **FIT** a pastry bag with a large star tip and fill ²/₃ full with the dough.

8   **DAB** a small amount of dough in each corner of a baking sheet and place a sheet of parchment paper on top. The dough will anchor the paper.

9   **PIPE** the dough into thick, 2-inch-long (5-cm) fingers, an inch (2.5 cm) apart.

10 **BAKE** in the oven for 15 minutes. Reduce the heat to 375°F (190°C) and bake for another 15 minutes.

11 **REMOVE** from the oven and let cool on the baking sheet.

12 **SERVE** at room temperature.

Baked Le Noble Cheese with Caramelized Onions & Sun-Dried Tomatoes, *page 90*

APPETIZERS

Baked Le Noble Cheese
with Caramelized Onions & Sun-Dried Tomatoes *(pictured on page 88)*

Using Le Noble cheese, formerly named Les Prés de Bayonne, produced by Fromagerie Domaine Féodal in Berthierville, QC.

Depending on the occasion, this dish can be served as an hors d'oeuvre, appetizer, or main course. If there are any leftovers, I would be tempted to eat it as a midnight snack. When I tested this recipe on Joanne, she said she would be very happy to skip the other two dishes planned for supper and just continue eating this one.

¼	cup (60 mL) unsalted butter
4	large onions, sliced
1	Tbsp (15 mL) chopped fresh thyme
4	cloves garlic, minced
½	cup (125 mL) dry white wine
2	lb (1 kg) Le Noble cheese, top rind removed
1	oz (25 g) sun-dried tomatoes, soaked in warm water
•	parsley sprig, for garnish
2	baguettes, sliced

TONY'S SUGGESTIONS
- ACIDIC WHITE WINE
  Pinot Grigio, Gavi, Aligoté
- MEDIUM-BODIED, DRY
  RED WINE
  Chianti, Barbera, Valpolicella, Ontario/BC Gamay
- DRY ROSÉ
- BEER
  Blanche (light-bodied white beer)

MAKE AHEAD
- *Onion mixture can be cooked 2 days ahead, covered, and refrigerated.*

GURTH'S NOTES
- *Use other similar soft, bloomy rind cheese such as brie, Camembert, Riopelle de l'Isle, Chevrotina, or Snow Road.*

Cooking Instructions

1   **IN A VERY LARGE SKILLET** or a wok, melt the butter over medium-high heat.

2   **COOK** the onions for 6 minutes or until just tender. Add the thyme.

3   **REDUCE** the temperature to medium and continue cooking until the onions are golden, about 30 minutes, stirring regularly.

4   **ADD** the garlic and cook for 1 minute. Pour in the wine and stir until the wine is nearly evaporated. Remove from the heat and let cool.

5   **PREHEAT** the oven to 350°F (180°C) and place the oven rack in the middle position.

6   **PLACE** the cheese in a large, oiled pie pan.

7   **PLACE** the caramelized onions over the top of the cheese.

8   **DRAIN** and slice the tomatoes. Place them in the centre of the onions.

9   **PLACE** on a baking sheet and bake in the oven for 15 to 20 minutes, or until the cheese begins to melt.

10 **TRANSFER** the pie pan onto a platter. Garnish the centre of the cheese with the parsley. Arrange baguette slices around the pan.

Broccoli Potage
with Marquis de Témiscouata

Using Marquis de Témiscouata, produced by Fromagerie Le Détour in Notre-Dame-du-Lac, QC.

Joanne said I should have a broccoli soup recipe in my book. A smart husband listens to his wife. Cooking a large amount of broccoli in a small amount of stock ensures the puréed soup is thick, without using any cream. The cheese thickens the soup a bit as well. Gurth is happy, for Joanne is happy!

1	Tbsp (15 mL) unsalted butter
1	onion, coarsely chopped
3	cloves garlic, minced
½	cup (125 mL) dry white wine
4	cups (1 L) chicken or vegetable stock
4	cups (1 L) broccoli, florets and peeled, sliced stems
1	sheet puff pastry, thawed
1	egg, lightly beaten with 1 Tbsp (15 mL) water
4	oz (100 g) Marquis de Témiscouata, rind removed

TONY'S SUGGESTIONS
- MEDIUM-BODIED, DRY WHITE WINE
  Sauvignon Blanc, unoaked Chardonnay, Arbois, Château-Chalon
- FORTIFIED WINE
  Palo Cortado or dry Oloroso sherry

MAKE AHEAD
- *Soup can be made to step 5 two days ahead, covered, and refrigerated. Reheat the soup before finishing.*

GURTH'S NOTES
- *Use other soft, bloomy rind cheese such as Ramembert, Camembert, White Moon, Comox Camembert, Island Bries, Bliss, goat brie, Madawaska Creemore.*

Cooking Instructions

1 **IN A LARGE SAUCEPAN,** melt the butter over medium-low heat. Add the onion, cover, and cook for 5 to 7 minutes, or until softened.

2 **ADD** the garlic and cook for 1 minute.

3 **POUR** in the wine, increase the heat to maximum, and cook until the wine has reduced by half.

4 **ADD** the stock and broccoli. Bring to a boil, reduce the heat, and simmer for 20 minutes, or until the broccoli is tender.

5 **WORKING IN BATCHES,** purée the soup in a blender. Transfer puréed soup back to the saucepan.

6 **PREHEAT** the oven to 425°F (220°C) and place the rack in the centre position Assemble 4 round 1-cup (250-mL) ramekins.

7 **ON A LIGHTLY FLOURED SURFACE,** roll the dough to ¼-inch (6-mm) thickness. Cut out 4 circles from the puff pastry, making them a bit larger than the tops of the ramekins.

8 **LADLE** the soup into the ramekins.

9 **BRUSH** the egg mixture along the rim of each ramekin.

10 **SHRED** the cheese and divide equally amongst the 4 bowls.

11 **COVER** the top of each ramekin with the puff pastry and lightly press onto the rim.

12 **BRUSH** the top of the puff pastry with the egg mixture.

13 **POKE** a hole in the dough to permit the steam from the soup to escape.

14 **PLACE** in the oven and bake for 10 minutes, or until the pastry is golden.

Cheddary Corn Chowder
with Smoked Trout

Using Bright 4-year-old Cheddar, produced by Bright Cheese and Butter Manufacturing Co. in Bright, ON.

Culinary legend has it that the word "chowder" comes from the French chaudière, meaning a pail, bucket, or cauldron. Fishermen used to make themselves a hearty stew with the fish they had recently caught. Obviously, farmers borrowed the idea and added their fresh corn, locally made cheddar, and some smoked fish.

2	Tbsp (30 mL) unsalted butter
1	onion, coarsely chopped
3	cloves garlic, coarsely chopped
2	Tbsp (30 mL) all-purpose flour
3	cups (750 mL) vegetable stock, at room temperature
1	potato, coarsely chopped
2	cups (500 mL) milk
1	cup (250 mL) half-and-half cream
2	cups (500 mL) frozen corn kernels
3	oz (75 g) smoked trout, coarsely chopped
1	green onion, sliced
4	oz (100 g) Bright 4-year-old Cheddar, crumbled
•	kosher salt and freshly ground black pepper, to taste

TONY'S SUGGESTIONS
- **WHITE WINE**
  Oak-aged Chardonnay from California, Ontario, BC, or Australia; white Bordeaux, white Rhône
- **FORTIFIED WINE**
  Sercial (dry Madeira)

MAKE AHEAD
- *Make the chowder up to step 6 a day ahead, cover, and refrigerate. Reheat before finishing the soup; reheating will cause the potatoes to break down and produce a thicker chowder.*

GURTH'S NOTES
- *Use your favourite local aged cheddar or Gouda in this recipe.*

Cooking Instructions

1 **IN A SOUP POT,** melt the butter over medium-low heat. Add the onions, cover, and cook for 5 to 7 minutes, or until softened.

2 **ADD** the garlic and cook for 2 minutes, stirring frequently.

3 **STIR** in the flour and cook for 1 minute.

4 **WHISK** in the stock gradually to ensure no lumps form.

5 **ADD** the potatoes and increase the heat to maximum. Cook until the potatoes are just tender, approximately 10 to 15 minutes.

6 **REDUCE** the temperature to a simmer and add the milk, cream, and corn kernels. Cook until heated through.

7 **MIX** in the trout, green onion, and cheese.

8 **SEASON** with salt and pepper, and serve before the cheese has completely melted.

PREPARATION TIME 30 MINS
COOKING TIME 90 MINS
MAKES 4 SERVINGS

Garlic Oka Gratinée Soup

Using Oka Classique, produced by Agropur in Montreal, QC.

Several years ago, I was invited to demonstrate cooking with garlic at the Garlic is Great! Festival in Milton, ON. This recipe was the result. It has become a favourite with both family and friends. Joanne and I love it for the amount of garlic and Oka cheese used. Don't panic about 2 whole garlic bulbs! When roasted it has a sweet and nutty taste. It's a delicious soup for the fall and winter season! Go to page 27 for directions on how to roast garlic.

1	Tbsp (15 mL) olive oil
2	bulbs garlic, cloves separated, peeled, roasted, and crushed
1	cup (250 mL) dry white wine
4	cups (1 L) chicken or vegetable stock
1	cup (250 mL) 35% cream
•	kosher salt and freshly ground black pepper, to taste
3	cloves garlic, peeled and sliced in half
4	slices rye bread, toasted
½	lb (250 g) Oka Classique cheese, grated
4	Tbsp (60 mL) cream sherry

TONY'S SUGGESTIONS
- **VIN JAUNE**
  Château Chalon
- **FORTIFIED WINE**
  Sherry: Palo Cortado or Oloroso, Verdelho (Madeira)
- **BEER**
  Spiced ale

MAKE AHEAD
- *Soup can be made to step 4, two days ahead, covered, and refrigerated.*
- *Garnish with cheese and croutons just prior to broiling and serving.*

GURTH'S NOTES
- *If Oka is not available, use a good stringy cheese, such as Saint-Paulin, Gouda, mozzarella, or Swiss.*

Garlic Oka Gratinée Soup (continued)
Cooking Instructions

1 **HEAT** the oil in a large soup pot over medium-low heat and add the crushed roasted garlic; cook for 1 minute.

2 **POUR** in the wine and bring to a boil. Cook until the volume has reduced by half.

3 **ADD** the stock and simmer for 15 minutes. Remove from the heat and let cool for 5 minutes.

4 **PURÉE** in a blender or food processor until smooth. Return the soup to the pot and place over medium-low heat. Stir in the cream. Season with salt and pepper.

5 **RUB** the garlic halves over the toasted bread and the inside surface of the soup bowls.

6 **PLACE** ⅛ of the cheese in each of the 4 bowls. Ladle 1 cup (250 mL) of soup into each bowl.

7 **PREHEAT** the oven to broil and place the oven rack in the top third position.

8 **POUR** 1 Tbsp (15 mL) of the sherry into each bowl. Cover with a slice of bread. Sprinkle the remaining cheese over the bread, and broil until the cheese is bubbling and slightly browned.

PREPARATION TIME 30 MINS
COOKING TIME 20 MINS
MAKES 4 SERVINGS

Forest Mushrooms Brioche
with Balderson Royal Canadian Cheddar

Using Balderson Royal Canadian Cheddar, produced by Balderson Cheese Ltd. in Lanark, ON.

Michael and Anna Olson, of Olson Food Concepts, created this recipe for Balderson Cheese Ltd. Use a mixture of mushrooms, such as oyster, shiitake, and portobello.

1	Tbsp (15 mL) unsalted butter
4	cups (1 L) mixed mushrooms, cleaned and cut into quarters or slices
•	kosher salt, to taste
2	Tbsp (30 mL) finely diced shallot or onion
½	Tbsp (7 mL) fresh thyme leaves
1	clove garlic, minced
¼	cup (60 mL) white wine
1	cup (250 mL) 35% cream
½	cup (125 mL) shredded Balderson Royal Canadian Cheddar
4	slices egg bread, toasted
4	thyme sprigs, for garnish

TONY'S SUGGESTIONS
- **OAK-AGED WHITE WINE**
  Chardonnay from California, Australia, or Chile
- **BOLD, NEW WORLD RED WINE**
  California Cabernet Sauvignon, Zinfandel, red Bordeaux, BC Merlot
- **BEER**
  Brown ale, India Pale Ale

MAKE AHEAD
- *Mushroom sauce can be made two days ahead, covered, and refrigerated.*

GURTH'S NOTES
- *Use your favourite local old or extra-old cheddar, Gouda, Swiss, brick, or farmer's cheese, if Balderson's isn't available in your region.*

Cooking Instructions

1 **MELT** the butter in a medium-sized pan over high heat until it foams. Add the mushrooms and a pinch of salt, and stir for 3 minutes until they start to soften.

2 **ADD** the shallot and thyme and stir for 1 minute. Add the garlic.

3 **ADD** the wine, cream, and cheese. Cook until it's reduced by half and has a sauce-like consistency.

4 **ADJUST** the salt to taste and spoon over the toasted bread, being sure to get all the sauce out of the pan with a rubber spatula.

5 **DECORATE** each serving with a sprig of thyme.

PREPARATION TIME 15 MINS
COOKING TIME 30 MINS
MAKES 4 SERVINGS

Cream of Fiddleheads
with Chèvre-Noît

Using Chèvre-Noît, produced by Abbaye de Saint-Benoît-du-Lac in Saint-Benoît-du-Lac, QC.

Fiddleheads are the baby fronds of the ostrich fern. When small and tightly furled, they have a wonderful flavour. One of the first edible wild ingredients to be harvested in spring, they are very popular in the Maritimes, Quebec, and Ontario. If you buy fresh ones, make certain you soak them several times in cold water to remove the sand and dirt lodged between their scales.

1	Tbsp (15 mL) unsalted butter
2	shallots, diced
3	cloves garlic, minced
1	cup (250 mL) dry white wine
1	lb (500 g) frozen fiddleheads, thawed and rinsed in cold water
4	cups (1 L) chicken or vegetable stock
½	cup (125 mL) 35% cream
•	kosher salt and freshly ground black pepper, to taste
4	oz (100 g) Chèvre-Noît, crumbled

TONY'S SUGGESTIONS
- **MEDIUM-BODIED, DRY WHITE WINE**
  Sauvignon Blanc from the Loire, Ontario, or New Zealand; Muscadet, Soave
- **FORTIFIED WINE**
  Fino or Manzanilla sherry

MAKE AHEAD
- *Soup can be made 2 days ahead, covered, and refrigerated. Warm over low heat and garnish with the cheese just before serving.*

GURTH'S NOTES
- *Use other blue cheese, such as the monks' Ermite or Benedictine Bleu, or Geai Bleu, Lavender Blue, Blossom's Blue, Blue Chèvrotina, Stilton, or roquefort.*
- *If fiddleheads are not available, fresh local asparagus is a good substitute.*

Cooking Instructions

1 **IN A SOUP POT,** melt the butter over medium-low heat. Cook the shallots for
   3 minutes, covered.

2 **ADD** the garlic and cook for 1 minute.

3 **POUR** in the wine and increase the temperature to maximum. Boil until the wine
   has reduced by half.

4 **IN A SMALL SAUCEPAN,** bring 3 cups (750 mL) of water to a boil. Throw in a pinch
   of salt. Blanch 8 of the fiddleheads in boiling water for 1 to 2 minutes until al
   dente. Remove and place in an ice-water bath to stop the cooking. Set aside.

5 **POUR** the stock into the soup pot and add the remaining fiddleheads. Bring to a
   boil and reduce the temperature to a simmer. Cook the fiddleheads for 10 to
   15 minutes, or until tender.

6 **PURÉE** the soup in a blender, working in small batches. Return the puréed soup to
   the pot and add the cream.

7 **REHEAT** the soup and season with salt and pepper.

8 **DIVIDE** equally amongst 4 bowls, scattering the crumbled cheese overtop and
   garnishing each serving with 2 blanched fiddleheads.

Oyster & Le Corsaire Soup

Using Le Corsaire, produced by Entreprise de la Ferme Chimo Inc. in Gaspé, QC.

For special occasions, my parents would order a peck of fresh oysters from the Maritimes. My dad would shuck them in the kitchen, enjoying a few raw on the half shell to make sure they were good. My mom would broil the majority of them for us, mixed with her favourite toppings. Here's a different way for them to use their oysters. They tried it and liked it a lot.

3	dozen small to medium oysters in their liquor
4	cups (1 L) cold water
¼	cup (60 mL) unsalted butter
1	onion, coarsely chopped
1	stalk celery, roughly chopped
¼	cup (60 mL) all-purpose flour
1	cup (250 mL) dry white wine
½	tsp (2 mL) freshly ground white pepper
¼	cup (60 mL) 35% cream
¾	cup (175 mL) milk
½	lb (250 g) Le Corsaire, cut in small pieces
½	lb (250 g) bacon, fried and crumbled
•	kosher salt, to taste

TONY'S SUGGESTIONS
- **CRISPLY DRY WHITE WINE**
  Muscadet, Chablis
- **SPARKLING WINE**
  Brut
- **FORTIFIED WINE**
  Fino or Manzanilla sherry
- **BEER**
  Guinness

MAKE AHEAD
- *The soup base can be made 1 day ahead, covered, and refrigerated. Reheat the soup over medium-low temperature and proceed with steps 9 to 11.*

GURTH'S NOTES
- *You can use either fresh or canned oysters. If you don't want to shuck them yourself, ask your fishmonger to shuck them for you into a container, preserving the liquor.*
- *Use your favourite soft, bloomy rind cheese such as Fleurmier, Les Caprices des saisons, brie, Ramembert, or Le Noble.*

Cooking Instructions

1 **IN A LARGE CONTAINER,** combine the oysters and their liquor with the cold water. Cover and refrigerate for 60 minutes.

2 **STRAIN** the oysters and set aside. Reserve the liquid.

3 **IN A LARGE SKILLET,** melt the butter over low heat. Add the onion and celery and cook until tender, approximately 5 to 7 minutes.

4 **STIR** in the flour and cook for approximately 2 minutes.

5 **BRING** the wine to a boil in a separate small pan; cook until the volume has reduced by half.

6 **SLOWLY** drizzle the reserved oyster liquid into the butter/flour mixture, stirring all the while to make sure no lumps form.

7 **STIR** in the pepper.

8 **ADD** the cream; turn the heat to high and bring to a near-boil.

9 **REDUCE** the heat to a simmer; add the milk and cheese.

10 **POUR** in the reduced wine and add the reserved oysters. Cook for 3 minutes.

11 **STIR** in the bacon. Season with salt and more white pepper and serve.

Broiled Blossom's Blue Oysters

Using Blossom's Blue, produced by Moonstruck Organic Cheese Inc. on Salt Spring Island, BC.

Two people were my inspiration in creating this dish: my Mom and Julia Grace of Moonstruck Organic Cheese Inc. At New Year's, my mother served my father, Joanne, and me broiled oysters. What a delicious way to start off 2007! Upon tasting the saltiness of the oysters, I thought of the delicious blue cheese Julia produces on Salt Spring Island. The salty ocean mist coating the vegetation her Jersey cows feed on influences the flavour of the milk, giving the cheese a true Pacific taste.

2	Tbsp (30 mL) unsalted butter
1	shallot, finely diced
½	cup (125 mL) panko or fresh white breadcrumbs
2	oz (50 g) Blossom's Blue, crumbled
12	oysters, shucked, on the half shell

Cooking Instructions

1 **IN A SMALL SKILLET,** melt the butter over medium-low heat. Cook the shallot for 3 minutes or until softened.

2 **REMOVE** the skillet from the heat. Add the panko and cheese, mix well.

3 **PLACE** the oven rack at the second-highest position and preheat the oven to broil.

4 **TOP** the shucked oysters with the cheese mixture and place on a baking sheet.

5 **BROIL** until the cheese has melted and the crumbs are golden, approximately 2 or 3 minutes. Serve this tasty BC treat immediately.

TONY'S SUGGESTIONS
- **WHITE WINE**
Muscadet, Jura white, Vernaccia di San Gimignano
- **CHAMPAGNE**
Brut or a very dry sparkler
- **FORTIFIED WINE**
Manzanilla sherry
- **BEER**
Guinness

MAKE AHEAD
- *Topping mixture can be made a day before, covered, and refrigerated.*

GURTH'S NOTES
- *The prep time all depends how good an oyster shucker you are. Invite someone who is and your prep is done in less than 12 minutes.*
- *Panko are Japanese breadcrumbs, available at good food shops, fishmongers, and Asian markets. They're coarser than regular breadcrumbs and provide a crunchy topping.*
- *Use your favourite crumbly blue cheese, such as Beddis Blue, Tiger Blue, Bleu Bénédictine, Rassembleu, Ciel de Charlevoix, Geai Bleu, Dragon's Breath, Stilton, or roquefort.*

Six-Vegetable Chowder
with Gouda

Using Herb and Garlic Gouda, produced by Cheeselady's Gouda Cheese in Winsloe North, PEI.

This soup is a delicious way to boost your daily vegetable intake. It's also a great way to clear out the fridge. Experiment with the vegetables you have in your crisper and make it taste good.

2	Tbsp (30 mL) unsalted butter
1	medium onion, chopped
1	bulb garlic, cloves peeled and cut in half
¼	cup (60 mL) all-purpose flour
4	+ ½ cups (1.1 L) chicken or vegetable stock
1	cup (250 mL) chopped cauliflower
1	cup (250 mL) chopped broccoli
1	cup (250 mL) chopped carrot
3	stalks celery, chopped
2	cups (500 mL) milk
1	+ ½ cups (375 mL) grated Herb and Garlic Gouda
•	kosher salt and freshly ground black pepper, to taste

TONY'S SUGGESTIONS
- MEDIUM-BODIED, DRY WHITE WINE
  White Burgundy, German dry Riesling, Ontario or BC Chardonnay (oaked)
- RED WINE
  Beaujolais-Villages, red Bordeaux
- FORTIFIED WINE
  Palo Cortado, dry Oloroso sherry
- BEER
  Belgian, porter

MAKE AHEAD
- *Cut all your vegetables ahead of time, cover, and refrigerate.*

GURTH'S NOTES
- *Herb mozzarella, herb havarti, Edam, or Esrom could be substituted for the Gouda.*

Cooking Instructions

1   **IN A LARGE SOUP POT,** melt the butter over medium-low heat.

2   **ADD** the onions, cover, and cook for 5 to 7 minutes, or until softened.

3   **ADD** the garlic and cook for 3 minutes.

4   **STIR** in the flour and cook for 1 minute.

5   **DRIZZLE** in the stock slowly, stirring all the while to ensure no lumps form.

6   **ADD** the cauliflower, broccoli, carrot, and celery.

7   **BRING** to a boil, reduce the heat to a simmer, and cover. Cook until the vegetables are tender, approximately 20 minutes.

8   **STIR** in the milk and continue to cook for 3 minutes.

9   **STIR** in the cheese and season with salt and pepper.

10   **SERVE** in warm bowls.

Caramelized Onion, Walnut
& Bleu de la Moutonnière Pizzenta

Using Bleu de la moutonnière, produced by Fromagerie la moutonnière in Sainte-Hélène-de-Chester, QC.

What is a pizzenta you ask? It's a pizza with a polenta crust. One night Joanne and I were craving a homemade pizza but didn't have the ingredients to make pizza dough. From necessity comes invention, and we had the makings for a firm polenta, which took less time to make and used fewer ingredients than the traditional dough. We first tasted this combination of caramelized onions, walnuts, and blue cheese on a pizza my sister Elena made for us at her home in the West Island of Montreal.

TONY'S SUGGESTIONS
- **MEDIUM-DRY WHITE WINE**
  Vouvray, Riesling Spätlese
- **BOLD RED WINE**
  Zinfandel, Primitivo, Amarone
- **BEER**
  Cherry, Nut Brown

MAKE AHEAD
- *Polenta and caramelized onions can be prepared a day ahead, covered, and refrigerated. Bring to room temperature before finishing in the oven.*

GURTH'S NOTES
- *Substitute another semi-soft blue cheese, such as Ermite, Rassembleu, Highland Blue, Geai Bleu, or Blossom's Blue.*

2	cups (500 mL) vegetable stock
²/₃	cup (150 mL) fine cornmeal
1	tsp (5 mL) dried basil
¼	tsp (1 mL) kosher salt
3	Tbsp (45 mL) extra virgin olive oil
2	white onions, finely sliced
¾	cup (175 mL) walnut pieces, toasted
7	oz (175 g) Bleu de la moutonnière, rind removed, crumbled
•	parsley sprigs, for garnish

Cooking instructions continued on following page . . .

Caramelized Onion, Walnut & Bleu de la Moutonnière Pizzenta (continued)
Cooking Instructions

1   IN a medium-sized saucepan, bring the stock to a boil.

2   WHISK in the cornmeal gradually.

3   REDUCE the heat to medium-low and add the basil and salt; continue to cook for 5 to 7 minutes, stirring with a wooden spoon.

4   GREASE an 11- x 16½-inch (27.5- x 42.5-cm) rectangular rimmed baking sheet. Pour the polenta into it and spread it over the sheet. Allow to cool to room temperature.

5   IN A LARGE SKILLET over medium-low temperature, heat 2 Tbsp (30 mL) of the oil.

6   ADD the onions and cook for 35 to 45 minutes, or until they are golden, stirring occasionally. Remove from the heat.

7   PLACE an oven rack in the second-highest position and set the oven to broil.

8   BROIL the polenta for 5 to 10 minutes, until the surface is firmer and light brown. Remove from the oven.

9   SET the oven to 350°F (180°C) and place the oven rack in the second-lowest position.

10   BRUSH the remaining 1 Tbsp (15 mL) oil on the top of the polenta.

11   SPREAD the onions evenly over the surface. Top with the walnuts and cheese.

12   BAKE for 10 to 12 minutes, or until the cheese has melted and the onions are warm.

13   CUT into 8 pieces, plate, and garnish each with a sprig of parsley.

PREPARATION TIME 10 MINS
COOKING TIME 40 MINS
MAKES 6 SERVINGS

The Waring House Apple Cider & Old Cheddar Soup

Using Old Cheddar, produced by Empire Cheese and Butter Co-operative in Campbellford, ON.

Executive Chef Luis de Sousa of The Waring House Restaurant & Inn in Picton, Ontario, created this recipe. Chef de Sousa scored big points with me when I saw this soup on his menu. Apple cider and cheese–two more of my favourite ingredients. His soup was a great starter to a delicious meal in the inn's Garden Dining Room.

2	+ ¾ cups (675 mL) water
½	large onion
3–4	stalks celery
1	large carrot
1	+ ⅓ cups (325 mL) sweet apple cider
⅔	cup (150 mL) maple syrup
2	Tbsp (30 mL) cornstarch
½	lb (250 g) Old Cheddar, shredded
1	+ ⅓ cups (325 mL) 35% cream
•	kosher salt and freshly ground black pepper, to taste

TONY'S SUGGESTIONS
- **APPLE CIDER**
  The same used in the soup
- **MEDIUM-BODIED WHITE WINE WITH SOME RESIDUAL SUGAR**
  Vouvray, Alsace Gewurztraminer, Semi-Dry Riesling from Ontario
- **FORTIFIED WINE**
  Oloroso sherry
- **SPIRITS**
  Calvados

MAKE AHEAD
- *Soup can be made 2 days ahead, covered, and refrigerated. Reheat over medium temperature until warm, about 10 to 15 minutes.*

GURTH'S NOTES
- *For a stronger flavour, use a nippy cheddar, such as a 2-, 3-, or 4-year-old.*

Cooking Instructions

1 **IN A LARGE STOCKPOT**, bring 2½ cups (625 mL) of the water, onion, celery, and carrot to a boil.

2 **SIMMER** for 15 to 20 minutes. Remove the vegetables and strain.

3 **ADD** the apple cider and maple syrup to the flavoured water.

4 **IN A MEASURING CUP**, dissolve the cornstarch in the remaining ¼ cup (60 mL) of water and stir into the soup. Heat until slightly thickened.

5 **STIR** in the cheese and cream. Season with salt and pepper.

6 **HEAT** gently until the cheese has melted and the soup is warm enough to serve.

Baked Courgettes
with Lemon & Pepper Okanagan Goat Cheese

Using Lemon and Pepper Okanagan Goat Cheese, produced by Happy Days Goat Dairy in Salmon Arm, BC.

Zucchini are also known as courgettes. This dish makes a great first course, but can also be served for lunch with a bowl of soup or a panini sandwich. I can imagine enjoying it with friends outside on the patio as part of a Sunday brunch. Joanne and I tested this recipe on our friends Paul and Helga. They said it was a keeper.

4	small zucchini cut in half lengthwise
2	Tbsp (30 mL) extra virgin olive oil
1	small onion, peeled and sliced into thin rounds
1	tsp (5 mL) herbes de Provence
•	kosher salt and freshly ground black pepper, to taste
8	oz (200 g) Lemon and Pepper Okanagan Goat Cheese
1	Tbsp (15 mL) 35% cream
2	Tbsp (30 mL) fresh basil, cut into very thin strips (chiffonade)
•	finely sliced radicchio, for garnish

TONY'S SUGGESTIONS
- MEDIUM-BODIED, CRISP DRY WHITE WINE
  BC Sauvignon Blanc or Sauvignon from the Loire, New Zealand, Ontario; unoaked Chardonnay, Muscadet
- BEER
  Belgian

MAKE AHEAD
- A day before, zucchini shells can be blanched and cooled, zucchini pulp and onions cooked, and cheese paste prepared; cover and refrigerate.

GURTH'S NOTES
- Use your favourite chèvre or cream cheese, plain or flavoured.

Cooking Instructions

1 **USING** a small melon baller, scoop out the inside of each zucchini half. Chop the pulp and set aside.

2 **BRING** a large pot of salted water to a boil. Blanch the zucchini shells until just tender, approximately 5 minutes. Immediately transfer the shells to a bowl of ice water to stop the cooking. Drain and set aside.

3 **IN A SMALL SKILLET,** heat the olive oil over medium-low temperature. Add the onions, cover, and cook until softened, about 3 to 5 minutes.

4 **ADD** the chopped zucchini and the herbes de Provence and continue to cook for 3 minutes, or until tender. Season with salt and pepper.

5 **PREHEAT** the oven to 400°F (200°C) and place the oven rack in the centre position. Oil a roasting pan.

6 **PLACE** the goat cheese and cream in a food processor and purée to form a paste.

7 **PLACE** the zucchini shells close together in the roasting pan. Fill each shell halfway with the onion/zucchini mixture.

8 **TOP** with the cheese paste and garnish with the basil.

9 **BAKE** for 15 minutes, or until the zucchini shells are soft. Remove and let cool for 3 minutes.

10 **SERVE** on a platter with a nest of sliced radicchio beneath it.

Pork Tenderloin & Cendré des prés Strudel, *page 118*

MAIN COURSES

Tiger Blue-Topped, Serrano Ham-Wrapped Filet Mignon, *page 136*

Pork Tenderloin & Cendré des prés Strudel

(pictured on page 114)

Using Le Cendré des prés, produced by Fromagerie Domaine Féodal in Berthierville, QC.

This recipe comes from the files of Lise Mercier, co-owner of Fromagerie Domaine Féodal. I prepared this dish for members of my Guinea Pig Club (i.e., my recipe tasters). They all loved it! Thank you, Lise, for sharing your delicious recipe with us.

1	pork tenderloin
•	kosher salt and freshly ground black pepper, to taste
⅓	cup (75 mL) unsalted butter
1	Tbsp (15 mL) extra virgin olive oil
1	Tbsp (15 mL) pesto
5	oz (125 g) Le Cendré des prés, sliced and rind removed
3	sheets phyllo dough

TONY'S SUGGESTIONS

- **OFF-DRY WHITE WINE**
  Riesling, California Chardonnay
- **LIGHTER-BODIED, FRUITY RED WINE**
  Beaujolais, Ontario/BC Pinot Noir, red Burgundy
- **SPARKLING WINE**
- **FORTIFIED WINE**
  Palo Cortado, dry Oloroso
- **BEER**
  Pilsner

MAKE AHEAD

- *Tenderloin can be prepared to the roasting stage 4 hours ahead, covered, and refrigerated*

GURTH'S NOTES

- *Try using chopped, sun-dried tomatoes in place of the pesto.*
- *Use any Canadian soft, bloomy rind cheese such as a brie or Camembert.*

Cooking Instructions

1 **PREHEAT** the oven to 375°F (190°C) and place the oven rack in the centre position. Line a baking sheet with parchment paper.

2 **SPRINKLE** salt and pepper on all sides of the pork tenderloin.

3 **IN A MEDIUM-SIZED SKILLET,** melt 1 Tbsp (15 mL) of the butter with the olive oil over medium heat.

4 **SEAR** the tenderloin until browned on all sides, approximately 3 to 4 minutes per side. Remove from the pan and let cool.

5 **BUTTERFLY** the pork tenderloin from end to end (to butterfly, cut it almost all the way through and open it like a book). Spread pesto in the cavity.

6 **PLACE** the cheese slices over the pesto. Close it up to enclose the filling. Set aside.

7 **IN A SMALL SKILLET,** melt the remaining butter.

8 **PLACE** a sheet of phyllo dough on a clean work surface. Keep the remaining sheets covered with a clean, dry tea towel.

9 **LIGHTLY** brush the phyllo sheet with melted butter. Place the second sheet on top, brush with butter, and repeat with the remaining phyllo.

10 **PLACE** the tenderloin towards the bottom of the long side of the phyllo sheets. Roll the phyllo over the tenderloin to enclose it, roll it one more time, then tuck in the outside edges of the dough and continue rolling. Seal the seam with melted butter and brush the entire strudel with butter.

11 **PUT** the wrapped tenderloin on the prepared baking sheet.

12 **ROAST** in the preheated oven for 15 minutes, or until the pastry is golden brown.

Bison & Chanterelle Stroganoff à la Maudite
with Asiago Spaetzle

In 2006, I worked as the Chef in the Canadian Pavilion at a huge Paris food trade show with Roger Provencher of Prairie Bison Meats and Terry Helary of Northern Lights Foods. Their Saskatchewan bison meat and chanterelle mushrooms are delicious. On a cold wintry day, I decided to create a Saskatchewan version of the classic Beef Stroganoff. Quebec and BC products are also used in this scrumptious dish. See if you can find them.

½	cup (125 mL) dried chanterelle mushrooms
2	cups (500 mL) hot water
1	lb (500 g) bison cubes
½	tsp (2 mL) kosher salt
¼	tsp (1 mL) freshly ground black pepper
¼	cup (60 mL) all-purpose flour
2	Tbsp (30 mL) butter
2	Tbsp (30 mL) olive oil
1	onion, thinly sliced
3	garlic cloves, minced
2	tsp (10 mL) tomato paste
1	bottle Maudite beer (12 oz/341 mL)
1	bay leaf

TONY'S SUGGESTIONS
- **FULL-BODIED, DRY RED WINE**
  Zinfandel, Australian Shiraz, Châteauneuf-du-Pape, Barolo, Amarone
- **FORTIFIED WINE**
  Tawny port
- **BEER**
  Bock

MAKE AHEAD
- *Stroganoff can be made several days ahead, covered, and refrigerated.*

GURTH'S NOTES
- *If bison is not available in your neck of the woods, beef, venison, caribou, or moose would be tasty substitutes.*
- *If your local beer store does not carry Quebec's La Maudite, your taste buds don't know what they're missing. You can substitute your favourite dark ale for my favourite beer.*

Cooking Instructions

1   **IN A MEDIUM BOWL,** soak the mushrooms in the hot water for 20 minutes.

2   **STRAIN** the liquid into another bowl and reserve. Chop the mushrooms coarsely.

3   **PLACE** the bison cubes in a large bowl and season with the salt and pepper. Add the flour and toss well so every piece of bison is coated.

4   **PLACE** a large saucepan over medium heat and melt the butter with the oil. Add the bison and brown the meat on all sides, about 5 to 7 minutes. Transfer the meat to a bowl.

5   **STIR** the onions into the saucepan, cover, and cook over medium-low heat for 5 to 7 minutes, or until softened.

6   **ADD** the garlic and cook for 1 minute.

7   **RETURN** the bison to the saucepan and stir in the tomato paste. Cook and stir for 1 minute.

8   **ADD** the chopped mushrooms, reserved mushroom broth, beer, and bay leaf.

9   **BRING** to a boil, then reduce the heat and simmer, partially covered, for 2 ½ hours. Stir occasionally and add a little water if the sauce is becoming too thick.

10 **REMOVE** the bay leaf and serve over fried Asiago Spaetzle.

Recipe continued on following page . . .

Bison & Chanterelle Stroganoff à la Maudite with Asiago Spaetzle (continued)

Asiago Spaetzle
Using Aged Asiago, produced by Jerseyland Organics in Grand Forks, BC.

3	eggs, lightly beaten
1	+ ½ cups (375 mL) breadcrumbs
½	tsp (2 mL) kosher salt
1	cup (250 mL) milk
¼	cup (60 mL) canola oil
3	oz (75 g) Asiago cheese, grated

MAKE AHEAD
- *Spaetzle can be prepared 2 days ahead, covered, and refrigerated. Reheat in a skillet over medium heat.*

GURTH'S NOTES
- *Try flavouring the spaetzle with toasted caraway, mustard or cumin seeds*
- *Aged Gouda, Montasio, Parmesan, or Sieur de Duplesiss would be good substitutes for the Asiago.*

Cooking Instructions

1 **FILL A LARGE SOUP POT** with water and bring to a simmer on the stove. Set a bowl of ice-cold water nearby.

2 **IN A LARGE BOWL**, mix the eggs, flour salt and milk to create a soft flowing batter.

3 **MEASURE** out ½ cup (125 ml) of the mixture and pour into a colander.

4 **USE** a rubber spatula to force the batter through the holes in the colander into the simmer water.

5 **WITH** a slotted spoon, gently stir the pasta for 2 to 3 minutes. Transfer the spaetzle to the cold water.

6 **REPEAT** with the remaining batter.

7 **DRAIN** the spaetzle and toss in a bowl with 2 tbsp (30 ml) of the oil.

8 **COVER** and refrigerate until required.

9 **PRIOR** to serving, heat a large skillet with 1 Tbsp (15 ml) of the oil to medium-high temperature. Add half of the spaetzle and pan-fry until slightly crispy. Transfer to a large bowl. Repeat with the remaining oil and spaetzle.

10 **TOSS** the spaetzle with the grated cheese.

11 **PLATE** and serve with the Stroganoff.

Bisonroni with Limburger

Using Limburger, produced by Oak Grove Cheese Factory Ltd. in New Hamburg, ON.

Hello everyone, this is Joanne. Gurth asked me to share with you one of my favourite types of recipes, a casserole. As a kid growing up in the '70s, I loved Beefaroni. Though my mother, Kathleen, sometimes gave in to my demands for Chef Boyardee, she also created a homemade version made with ground beef, cheddar cheese, and diced tomatoes. I always thought her version was the best. To this day, this simple recipe represents comfort food to me. This is a slightly more upscale version, using ground bison and Limburger cheese. I still make this dish when I want the comfort that only Mom can bring.

12	oz (300 g) pasta shells
2	Tbsp (30 mL) extra virgin olive oil
1	red onion, coarsely chopped
5	cloves of garlic, diced
1	lb (500 g) ground bison
1	28-oz (796-mL) can diced tomatoes
1	tsp (5 mL) dried thyme
10	oz (250 g) Limburger cheese, shredded

TONY'S SUGGESTIONS
- **A HEARTY RED WINE WITH GOOD ACIDITY**
  Chianti, Barbera, Valpolicella Ripasso, Ontario/BC Merlot, young red Bordeaux, Tempranillo, Côtes du Rhône
- **FORTIFIED WINE**
  Amontillado sherry
- **BEER**
  Real ale

MAKE AHEAD
- *The dish can be assembled to the baking stage a day ahead, covered, and refrigerated. Let warm up at room temperature for 30 minutes. Bake just prior to serving.*

JOANNE'S NOTES
- *This dish is just as tasty à la Kathleen—with the ground beef and cheddar.*
- *To reduce the chance of salmonella food poisoning, it's important to cook ground meat (whether it's beef, pork, turkey, veal, chicken, lamb, or bison) to well done; it should be grey or white through the centre. Salmonella bacteria survive on the surface of meat and ground meat has a very large surface area with all its little pieces.*

Cooking Instructions

1. **PREHEAT** the oven to 350°F (180°C) and place the oven rack in the centre position. Spray an 8-cup (2-L) baking dish with cooking spray.

2. **BRING** a large pot of salted water to a boil and cook the pasta until al dente, about 8 to 10 minutes.

3. **DRAIN** and cool with cold water. Drain the pasta and toss in a bowl with 1 Tbsp (15 mL) of the oil. Set aside.

4. **IN A LARGE SKILLET**, heat the remaining 1 Tbsp (15 mL) oil over medium-low temperature. Add the onion, cover, and cook for 5 minutes, or until tender.

5. **ADD** the garlic and cook for 1 minute.

6. **STIR** in the meat and brown well, about 10 minutes.

7. **STIR** in the tomatoes with their juice. Cook for 5 minutes.

8. **STIR** in the thyme.

9. **SPOON** ⅓ of the pasta into the bottom of the dish. Ladle ½ of the meat mixture over the pasta and sprinkle ⅓ of the grated cheese overtop.

10. **REPEAT** with another layer of pasta, meat, and cheese.

11. **ADD** the final layer of pasta and sprinkle with the remaining cheese.

12. **PLACE** the dish on a baking sheet and cook uncovered for 20 minutes.

13. **COOL** for 5 minutes before serving.

(top) Smoked Monterey Jack Cornbread Muffins, *page 129*

Mesquite Beef & Duck Sausage Stew

I love stews that have simmered for several hours on the stovetop. You walk into the house from the cold outside and you smell the aroma of that stew, oh yeah! Letting the stew simmer gives the meat a chance to braise and soften in the tasty broth. All the flavours mix together and create a deelicious, mouth-watering feast. Serve this with Smoked Monterey Jack Cornbread Muffins (page 129).

3	Tbsp (45 mL) mesquite seasoning mix
4	Tbsp (60 mL) all-purpose flour
1	lb (500 g) stewing beef, cubed, patted dry
¼	cup (60 mL) unsalted butter
1	large onion, sliced
4	cloves garlic, diced
7	cups (1.75 L) beef stock
3	duck sausages, steamed, sliced, and pan-fried
1	19-oz (594-mL) can romano beans, drained and rinsed
2	cups (500 mL) cherry tomatoes

Cooking instructions continued on following page . . .

TONY'S SUGGESTIONS
- **FULL-BODIED, DRY RED WINE**
  California Zinfandel, Australian Shiraz, Chilean Merlot, Argentinean Malbec, Amarone
- **FORTIFIED WINE**
  Oloroso sherry
- **BEER**
  Double bock

MAKE AHEAD
- *Stew can be made 2 days ahead, omitting the tomatoes, covered, and refrigerated. Bring to a simmer and add the tomatoes before serving.*

GURTH'S NOTES
- *Use your favourite style of sausage: venison, wild boar, lamb, Italian, or Bratwurst.*

Mesquite Beef & Duck Sausage Stew *(continued)*
Cooking Instructions

1 **IN A LARGE BOWL,** combine the spice mix and flour. Add the beef cubes and toss until they're well coated.

2 **IN A LARGE SOUP POT,** melt the butter over medium-high heat. Sear the cubes on all sides, approximately 4 minutes in total. Remove the meat from the pot and set aside.

3 **REDUCE** the temperature to medium-low and add the sliced onion to the pot. Cover and cook for 5 minutes.

4 **ADD** the garlic and cook for 1 minute.

5 **RETURN** the beef to the pot and cook for 2 minutes, stirring occasionally.

6 **DRIZZLE** the beef stock into the pot, stirring continuously.

7 **BRING** to a boil, reduce the heat to a simmer, and cook for 2 hours, uncovered.

8 **FIFTEEN MINUTES PRIOR TO SERVING,** add the sausage, beans, and tomatoes.

9 **LADLE** into individual bowls and enjoy with Smoked Monterey Jack Cornbread Muffins (recipe on next page.)

Smoked Monterey Jack Cornbread Muffins

(pictured on page 126)

Using Smoked Monterey Jack, produced by Ivanhoe Cheese in Ivanhoe, ON.

¾ cup (175 mL) cornmeal

1 cup (250 mL) all-purpose flour

1 Tbsp (15 mL) baking powder

½ tsp (2 mL) kosher salt

2 tsp (10 mL) brown sugar, packed

1 egg

1 cup (250 mL) milk

2 Tbsp (30 mL) unsalted butter, melted

2 Tbsp (30 mL) chopped sun-dried tomatoes,
 soaked in warm water and drained

2 green onions, sliced

¾ cup (175 mL) grated Smoked Monterey Jack

TONY'S SUGGESTIONS
- **FULL-BODIED WHITE**
 oak-aged chardonnay, Pinot Gris
- **FULL-BODIED ROSÉ**
 Tavel, Lirac
- **BEER**
 wheat ale, Pilsner

MAKE AHEAD
- *Make 1 to 2 days ahead, cover, and store at room temperature.*

GURTH'S NOTES
- *Substitute smoked Gouda, or a jalapeño or Cajun cheddar, for the Smoked Monterey Jack.*

Cooking Instructions

1 **PREHEAT** the oven to 425°F (220°C) and place the oven rack in the middle position. Grease or spray a standard-sized muffin tin with cooking oil.

2 **IN A MEDIUM BOWL,** combine the cornmeal, flour, baking powder, salt, and sugar, mixing well. Make a well in the centre.

3 **IN A SMALLER BOWL,** blend the egg and milk together. Stir in the melted butter, sun-dried tomatoes, green onion, and cheese.

4 **POUR** the wet ingredients into the well of the dry ingredients and stir just enough to moisten the dry ingredients.

5 **DIVIDE** the mixture among 9 of the muffin cups. Pour a little water in the remaining 3 empty cups.

6 **BAKE** in the preheated oven for 8 to 10 minutes, or until a toothpick inserted in the middle of a muffin comes out dry.

7 **REMOVE** from the oven and cool for 3 minutes before turning the muffins out and cooling on a rack.

Pistachio-Crusted Veal
stuffed with Bouq'Émissaire

Using Bouq'Émissaire, produced by Fromages Chaput in Châteauguay, QC.

I wanted to create a veal recipe that incorporated aspects of veal Parmesan with beef rouladen, minus the pickle. The strong goat and olivewood ash flavours of the Bouq'Émissaire give the dish a wonderful tanginess and make it even more memorable. After tasting my new dish, my tummy purred with contentment.

2	veal scaloppini (5 oz/125 g each)
2	tsp (10 mL) dried tarragon
3	oz (75 g) Bouq'Émissaire, halved
2	eggs, lightly beaten
⅓	cup (75 mL) all-purpose flour
⅔	cup (150 mL) salted pistachios, shelled and finely chopped
2	Tbsp (30 mL) unsalted butter
4	lemon wedges

Cooking instructions continued on following page . . .

TONY'S SUGGESTIONS
- **DRY WHITE WINE**
  Grüner Veltliner, Riesling Kabinett, or dry Riesling from Ontario; Sauvignon Blanc from the Loire
- **DRY RED WINE**
  Rioja red, Beaujolais, Ontario or BC Gamay
- **BEER**
  Pilsner

MAKE AHEAD
- *Prepare the veal rolls to the cooking stage a day ahead, cover, and refrigerate. Return to room temperature prior to cooking.*

GURTH'S NOTES
- *Joanne also likes this dish when I use Fromage Côté's Sir Laurier d'Arthabaska. You can also use brie, Oka, or dill Gouda.*

Pistachio-Crusted Veal stuffed with Bouq'Émissaire (continued)
Cooking Instructions

1   **PREHEAT** the oven to 350°F (180°C) and place the oven rack in the middle position.

2   **WORKING WITH 1 AT A TIME,** place the veal between 2 sheets of plastic wrap and use a food mallet to lightly pound it until it's 1/8 inch (3 mm) thick.

3   **SPRINKLE** 1 tsp (5 mL) of the tarragon over the flattened veal.

4   **PLACE** a chunk of cheese in the bottom 1/3 of the veal. Brush the edges of the veal with the beaten egg.

5   **ROLL** the veal up; when the cheese is enclosed, tuck the sides of the veal into the centre and continue to roll.

6   **DUST** the veal roll with the flour.

7   **DUNK** into the beaten eggs and roll in the chopped pistachios, coating the veal completely. Repeat with the remaining veal.

8   **MELT** the butter in a large ovenproof skillet over low heat and brush the veal rolls with the butter.

9   **PLACE** the veal rolls, seam-side down, in the warm skillet and roast in the oven for 10 to 12 minutes, or until the pistachios are golden.

10   **TRANSFER** the veal to individual plates and garnish with the lemon wedges.

Spaghetti with Meatballs Surprise

Using Onion Mozzarella, produced by Empire Cheese and Butter Co-operative in Campbellford, ON.

"On top of spaghetti, all covered with cheese, I lost my poor meatball, when somebody sneezed . . . " I used to sing this and many other Boy Scout songs when attending Jackson Dodds and Tamaracouta Scout camps in Quebec. If we had meatballs like the ones in this recipe, I wouldn't lose it.

2	shallots, finely diced
½	lb (250 g) ground beef
½	lb (250 g) ground pork
1	egg, beaten
1	tsp (5 mL) dried basil
1	tsp (5 mL) dried oregano
⅔	cup (150 mL) breadcrumbs
3	oz (75 g) Onion Mozzarella, cut into 12 cubes
6	cups (1.5 L) tomato sauce
1	lb (500 g) spaghetti noodles

Cooking Instructions

1 **IN A BOWL,** combine the shallots, beef, pork, egg, basil, oregano, and breadcrumbs.

2 **FORM** a small handful of the meat mixture into a patty. Place a piece of cheese in the centre of the patty, and form into a ball. Repeat with the remaining meat mixture and cheese, placing the meatballs in a container lined with waxed paper.

3 **REFRIGERATE,** covered, for 60 minutes.

4 **IN A SAUCEPAN,** heat the tomato sauce over medium-low heat. When it's gently bubbling, add the meatballs. Return to a simmer, cover, and cook for 60 minutes.

5 **BRING** a large pot of water to a boil, and cook the spaghetti until al dente. Drain.

6 **DIVIDE** the spaghetti amongst 4 plates. Top with the meatballs and tomato sauce and serve immediately.

TONY'S SUGGESTIONS
- **DRY RED WINE**
  Chianti, Barbera, Dolcetto, Rioja red, Ontario or BC Cabernet Sauvignon, Zinfandel
- **BEER**
  Belgian

MAKE AHEAD
- *Meatballs can be made 1 day ahead, covered, and refrigerated.*

GURTH'S NOTES
- *Cooking the meatballs in the tomato sauce gives both more flavour.*
- *Try using other flavoured cheeses. There are several flavoured Goudas, havartis, mozzarellas, and cheddars available.*

PREPARATION TIME 30 MINS
COOKING TIME 15 MINS
MAKES 2 SERVINGS

Gomashio-Coated Whitefish
with Wasabi Verdelait Soba Noodles

Using Wasabi Verdelait, produced by Natural Pastures Cheese Company in Courtenay, BC.

Gomashio is a mixture of toasted sesame seeds and salt that's often used to flavour Japanese cuisine. In this dish, I've used dried seaweed, nori, instead of salt. Nori is available in some supermarkets and in Asian food stores. Soba or Japanese buckwheat noodles can be found at these markets and at fine food stores. Besides making cheese, Natural Pastures Cheese Co. grows wasabi, a Japanese green horseradish that has quite the kick. If you want to cook with wasabi, use it sparingly and in very, very small doses. A very small pinch is enough for me. When eaten raw or in its paste form, you experience a very intense buzz for thirty seconds, your sinuses clear, and the effect quickly subsides. What a rush!

1	+ ½ tsp (7.5 mL) nori flakes
1	Tbsp (15 mL) black sesame seeds
1	Tbsp (15 mL) white sesame seeds, toasted
2	whitefish fillets
3	Tbsp (45 mL) unsalted butter, divided
2	Tbsp (30 mL) all-purpose flour
1	cup (250 mL) milk
4	oz (100 g) Wasabi Verdelait cheese, shredded
•	kosher salt and freshly ground white pepper, to taste
1	Tbsp (15 mL) extra virgin olive oil
2	shallots, finely diced
3	cloves of garlic, minced
4	large shiitake mushrooms, thinly sliced
1	piece fresh ginger (1 inch/2.5 cm), peeled and minced
2	oz (50 g) soba noodles, cooked

TONY'S SUGGESTIONS
- **OFF-DRY, AROMATIC WHITE WINE**
  Gewurztraminer, Riesling Spätlese, Viognier, white Zinfandel
- **SAKE**
- **FORTIFIED WINE**
  Fino sherry
- **BEER**
  Pale ale, lager

MAKE AHEAD
- *Sauce can be made a day ahead, cooled, covered, and refrigerated.*

GURTH'S NOTES
- *Wasabi Verdelait is a unique BC cheese. You could use an onion mozzarella, mild dill Gouda, or herb cheddar instead.*

Cooking Instructions

1 **IN A SMALL BOWL,** combine the nori and both kinds of sesame seeds.

2 **COAT** the fish fillets with the mixture. Set aside.

3 **IN A SAUCEPAN,** melt 2 Tbsp (30 mL) of the butter over medium-low heat. Stir in the flour and cook for 3 minutes.

4 **SLOWLY** drizzle in the milk, whisking constantly to prevent lumps from forming. Cook the sauce for 5 to 7 minutes, or until it begins to thicken.

5 **STIR** in the cheese and continue cooking until it all melts. Season with salt and white pepper.

6 **IN A MEDIUM SKILLET,** heat the oil over medium-low temperature. Add the shallots and cook for 3 minutes.

7 **ADD** the garlic, mushrooms, and ginger; cook for 3 to 4 minutes. Set aside and keep warm.

8 **IN A LARGE SKILLET,** melt the remaining 1 Tbsp (15 mL) butter over medium heat. Add the coated fish and cook for 3 to 5 minutes on each side, depending on the thickness of the fillets. They should be just warm when probed inside. If you cook it longer, the fish begins to flake and falls apart.

9 **IN A BOWL,** toss the cooked noodles with the cheese sauce.

10 **CREATE** a nest of noodles in the centre of each plate. Spoon the shiitake/shallot mixture over the noodles and top with the fillets.

Tiger Blue-Topped, Serrano Ham-Wrapped Filet Mignon

(pictured on page 117)

Using Tiger Blue, produced by Poplar Grove Wine and Cheese Inc. in Penticton, BC.

Blue cheese and filet mignon go so well together. The tanginess of the cheese gives an extra zip to this tender cut of beef. Whipped sweet potatoes with buttered Brussels sprouts make great side dishes. My mouth is watering as I am typing in this recipe. Serrano ham is a dry-cured Spanish ham that is generally served raw in thin slices, similar to Italian prosciutto. It is becoming more readily available at fine food shops and delis. If it's not available, use prosciutto, pancetta, jambon de Bayonne, or smoked bacon instead.

2	beef filet mignon (6 oz/150 g each)
•	kosher salt and freshly ground black pepper, to taste
2	slice Serrano ham, folded in half widthwise
2	Tbsp + 1 tsp (35 mL) unsalted butter
2	slices of Tiger Blue cheese
½	cup (125 mL) dry red wine

TONY'S SUGGESTIONS
- **FULL-BODIED RED WINE WITH SOME SWEETNESS**
  Amarone, California or Chilean Merlot, Argentinean Malbec
- **OFF-DRY WHITE WINE**
  German Riesling Spätlese, Ontario semi-dry Riesling, medium-dry Vouvray
- **FORTIFIED WINE**
  Amontillado sherry
- **BEER**
  Pale ale, dry porter

MAKE AHEAD
- *Filet mignon can be seasoned and wrapped with the ham a day ahead, covered, and refrigerated.*

GURTH'S NOTES
- *Use your favourite blue cheese, such as Blue Benedictine, Ciel de Charlevoix, Lavender Blue, Beddis Blue, Bleu de la moutonnière, Stilton, or roquefort.*

Cooking Instructions

1 **SEASON** the beef with salt and pepper.

2 **WRAP** each filet mignon with a piece of ham. Spear the ham into place with wooden toothpicks.

3 **PREHEAT** the oven to broil.

4 **IN A LARGE OVENPROOF SKILLET,** melt 2 Tbsp (30 mL) of the butter over medium-high heat. Add the beef and sear the top and bottom for 5 minutes each.

5 **PLACE** the slices of cheese on top of the meat and broil until the cheese is beginning to melt.

6 **TRANSFER** to a plate, cover, and let rest for 10 minutes.

7 **DEGLAZE** the pan with the red wine, scraping the bottom of the skillet with a wooden spoon to melt the caramelized beef bits into the wine. Cook until the volume has reduced by half.

8 **STRAIN** the jus into a bowl and stir in the remaining 1 tsp (5 mL) of butter until melted.

9 **REMOVE** the toothpicks from the beef, place on serving plates, and drizzle the red wine jus around the meat.

Creamy Pork Chops à la D'Iberville

Using D'Iberville cheese, produced by Fromagerie au Gré des Champs in Saint-Jean-sur-Richelieu, QC.

At first I was unsure if the flavour combination of pork chops, caramelized onions, cheese, cider vinegar, and mustard would work together. But when Joanne and I tested the recipe, we were tempted to lick the plate after devouring the yummy pork chop. My sister Elena and her family make visiting Fromagerie au Gré des Champs to purchase their organic and raw milk cheese part of a day's outing from their Dorval home. My nephews Jonathan and Shane prefer the D'Iberville, while Elena and her husband, Sébastien, enjoy Le Monnoir, a firm, mixed rind cheese.

3	Tbsp (45 mL) unsalted butter
1	onion, thinly sliced
3	oz (75 g) D'Iberville, rind removed and cubed
⅔	cup (150 mL) 35% cream
2	pork chops, 5 oz (125 g) each
•	kosher salt and freshly ground black pepper, to taste
3	Tbsp (45 mL) cider vinegar
2	tsp (10 mL) Dijon mustard

Cooking instructions continued on following page . . .

TONY'S SUGGESTIONS
- **OFF-DRY WHITE WINE**
  Riesling Spätlese, Alsace Gewurztraminer, California Chardonnay
- **MEDIUM-BODIED, DRY RED**
  Pinot Noir, light-bodied Zinfandel
- **BEER**
  Bock, German lager

MAKE AHEAD
- *Caramelized onions can be prepared a day ahead, covered, and refrigerated. Bring to room temp before continuing with the dish.*

GURTH'S NOTES
- *For really juicy, flavourful pork chops, use those that are cut close to the rib end.*
- *Pork can be cooked medium-rare. If you like it well done, cook the chops longer.*
- *Try this recipe with Oka, St-Paulin, Pied-de-vent, Gouda, or even havarti.*

Creamy Pork Chops à la D'Iberville (continued)
Cooking Instructions

1 **PREHEAT** the oven to 350°F (180°C) and place the oven rack in the centre position.

2 **IN A LARGE OVENPROOF SKILLET,** melt 1 Tbsp (15 mL) of the butter over medium heat. Add the onion and cook for 20 minutes, until lightly caramelized, stirring occasionally.

3 **IN A MIXING BOWL,** combine the cheese with ½ cup (125 mL) of the cream.

4 **TRANSFER** the onions to a bowl and set aside.

5 **USING THE SAME SKILLET,** melt the remaining 2 Tbsp (30 mL) butter over medium heat. Season both sides of the pork chops with salt and pepper and cook for 5 minutes. Turn the chops over.

6 **SPOON** the caramelized onions on top of the pork chops. Drizzle the cream and cheese mixture over the caramelized onions.

7 **PLACE** in the preheated oven and roast for 10 minutes.

8 **REMOVE** the skillet from the oven. Transfer the pork chops to a serving plate and cover with foil.

9 **POUR** the remaining butter/cream mixture out of the skillet into a bowl and set aside.

10 **PLACE** the skillet on the stovetop over medium-low temperature, and add the cider vinegar. With a wooden spoon, scrape the bottom and sides of the skillet to dissolve the bits of pork and juices.

11 **ADD** the remaining cream, the mustard, and the reserved butter/cream mixture. Continue to cook and stir until thickened, about 3 to 5 minutes.

12 **LADLE** the sauce over the pork chops and serve.

Greek Chicken Feta Ziti

Using Feta cheese, produced by Skotidakis Goat Farm in Saint-Eugène, ON.

This recipe comes from the files of John Skotidakis of Skotidakis Goat Farm. Joanne doubted the feta would melt enough to form a sauce when added to the cooked noodles. She was happily surprised and had seconds!

1	cup (250 mL) chicken stock
2	tsp (10 mL) dried oregano
1	lb (500 g) boneless, skinless chicken breasts, cut into ½-inch (1-cm) cubes
½	lb (250 g) dried ziti pasta
4	oz (100 g) Skotidakis Feta, crumbled
1	Tbsp (15 mL) lemon juice
1	tsp (5 mL) kosher salt
½	tsp (2 mL) freshly ground black pepper
3	Tbsp (45 mL) chopped fresh parsley
1	+ ½ cups (375 g) cherry tomatoes, halved

Cooking Instructions

1 **IN A LARGE SKILLET,** simmer the chicken stock and oregano until ½ cup (125 mL) of liquid remains, about 10 minutes.

2 **STIR** in the chicken, cover the pan, and cook for 5 to 7 minutes.

3 **BRING** a large pot of salted water to a boil and cook the ziti until just done, about 13 minutes.

4 **DRAIN** the pasta and toss it with the chicken, feta, lemon juice, salt, pepper, and parsley. Stir until the cheese is completely melted.

5 **TOSS** in the cherry tomatoes and serve immediately.

TONY'S SUGGESTIONS
- **DRY WHITE WINE**
  Greek white, Chablis, unoaked Chardonnay from Ontario or BC, Alsace Pinot Blanc
- **DRY ROSÉ WINE**
- **BEER**
  Lager

MAKE AHEAD
- *Use different styles of pasta, such as fusili or rotini, or pasta made from whole wheat or spelt flour.*

GURTH'S NOTES
- *Try it with other styles of cheese. Your favourite soft cheese with a bloomy rind (such as Camembert) would work well, too.*

Chorizo Moussaka

Using Duro Blanco cheese, produced by Portuguese Cheese Co. in Toronto, ON.

Joanne and I were inspired to make this dish after preparing and devouring a traditional Greek moussaka with ground lamb and eggplant. We both love good sausages and potatoes, so we incorporated them into a version of this classic dish. Like many other casserole dishes, you can prepare this one earlier in the day and bake it in the oven just prior to supper. Joanne likes this, for it gives us the opportunity to wash the used bowls and pans prior to supper.

¾	cup (175 mL) extra virgin olive oil
1	large onion, finely chopped
4	cloves garlic, chopped
5	chorizo sausages, casings removed
¼	tsp (1 mL) ground cinnamon
¼	tsp (1 mL) ground allspice
2	14-oz (400 g) cans chopped tomatoes
1	Tbsp (15 mL) chopped fresh oregano
2	bay leaves
1	tsp (5 mL) chopped fresh thyme leaves
2	medium eggplants, cut into ½-inch (1-cm) slices
3	Tbsp (45 mL) unsalted butter
3	Tbsp (45 mL) all-purpose flour
3	+ ½ cups (875 mL) milk
3	oz (75 g) Parmesan, grated
4	oz (100 g) Duro Blanco, grated
•	kosher salt and freshly ground black pepper, to taste
•	all-purpose flour, for dusting
3	potatoes, sliced
2	egg yolks
1	egg

TONY'S SUGGESTIONS
- **GUTSY RED WINE**
  Zinfandel, Primitivo, Greek Nemea, Côtes du Rhône, BC Shiraz, Australian Shiraz
- **BEER**
  Porter

MAKE AHEAD
- *This dish can be prepared up to the baking point in advance and refrigerated.*
- *Allow an extra 15 minutes in the oven if cooking from cold.*

GURTH'S NOTES
- *Use other firm cheese, such as Gouda, Emmenthal, or Gruyère.*
- *Use your favourite sausage, mild or spicy.*

Cooking Instructions

1 **IN A LARGE SKILLET,** heat 2 Tbsp (30 mL) of the olive oil over medium temperature. Add the onion, cover, and cook for 5 to 7 minutes, or until the onion is soft.

2 **ADD** the garlic and cook for 1 minute. Stir in the sausage meat, breaking it up with a fork, and cook for 5 minutes.

3 **MIX** in the cinnamon, allspice, tomatoes, oregano, bay leaves, and thyme. Reduce the heat and simmer for approximately 1 hour.

4 **PLACE** the eggplant in a colander, sprinkle with salt and let sit for 30 minutes. (This draws out any bitter juices.)

5 **MEANWHILE,** make the cheese sauce. Melt the butter in a saucepan over medium-low heat and stir in the flour. Cook and stir for 2 minutes.

6 **DRIZZLE** in the milk, whisking constantly to ensure no lumps form.

7 **SIMMER** over low heat for 5 to 8 minutes, whisking until the sauce thickens.

8 **REMOVE** from the heat and stir in ⅔ of the Parmesan and ½ of the Duro Blanco. Season with salt and pepper.

9 **PLACE** the remaining oil in a large skillet over medium-high heat. Rinse the eggplant, pat it dry, and dust with flour. Working in batches, fry until golden on both sides, about 8 to 10 minutes. Remove from the pan and set aside to drain on paper towels.

10 **WORKING IN BATCHES,** fry the potato slices in the same oil until lightly golden, about 8 to 10 minutes. Remove and drain on paper towels.

11 **THE CHEESE SAUCE SHOULD NOW** have cooled enough to whisk in the egg and egg yolks.

12 **PREHEAT** the oven to 350°F (180°C) and place the oven rack in the centre position. Place an 8- x 12-inch (20- x 30-cm) baking dish on a baking sheet.

13 **ARRANGE** the potato slices over the bottom of the dish. Spoon ⅓ of the onion/sausage mixture overtop, then cover with ½ of the eggplant slices. Repeat the layers, ending with the meat.

14 **POUR** the cheese sauce overtop. Sprinkle with the remaining Parmesan and Duro Blanco.

15 **BAKE** in the preheated oven for 50 to 60 minutes, until bubbling and golden.

16 **ALLOW** the moussaka to settle for 5 minutes before cutting into squares and serving.

Lamb Burgers
with a Dragon's Breath

Using Dragon's Breath, produced by That Dutchman's Farm in Upper Economy, NS.

I appear regularly on CTV's "Canada AM," demonstrating recipes featuring Canadian ingredients I discover during my travels. I surprise hosts Seamus O'Regan and Beverly Thomson with the cornucopia of Canadian goodies I bring with me. In June 2006, I was asked to show different barbecue sandwiches and this recipe, using Ontario lamb and blue cheese, was one of them. Seamus and Tom Brown, the weatherman, each took half of the burger. At another appearance, Beverly's favourite Canadian cheese was the Dragon's Breath.

1	tsp (5 mL) ground rosemary
1	tsp (5 mL) dried oregano
1	lb (500 g) ground lamb
½	cup (125 mL) diced red onions
¼	cup (60 mL) breadcrumbs
1	egg, beaten
8	oz (200 g) Dragon's Breath cheese

Cooking Instructions

1 **IN A SMALL BOWL,** combine the rosemary, oregano, lamb, onions, and breadcrumbs.

2 **ADD** the beaten egg and mix well.

3 **DIVIDE** the cheese into 4 equal portions and roll each piece into a ball.

4 **FORM** the meat into 4 patties. Place a piece of cheese in the middle of each patty. Cover the cheese with the meat and re-form into a patty.

5 **PLACE** the patties on a plate. Cover with plastic wrap and refrigerate for 1 hour.

6 **PREHEAT** the grill to medium and cook the patties until well done, for 5 to 7 minutes on each side, or until the meat is cooked through.

TONY'S SUGGESTIONS
- **FULL-BODIED RED WINE WITH SOME SWEETNESS**
  Amarone, Zinfandel, Primitivo, Chilean Merlot, Argentinean Malbec
- **FORTIFIED WINE**
  Tawny port, Oloroso sherry
- **BEER**
  Barley wine

MAKE AHEAD
- *Patties can be made to the grilling stage 1 day ahead, covered, and refrigerated (add cooking time for refrigeration factor).*

GURTH'S NOTES
- *Try this with ground chicken, turkey, veal, or pork.*
- *Use other blue cheese, such as Borgonzola, Bleu de la moutonnière, or Highland Blue.*
- *You could also use a semi-soft, washed rind cheese, such as Cru des Érables, Limburger, or Monterey Jack.*

Potato, Sausage & Onion Pie

Using La Chute Chaudière Cheddar, produced by Fromagerie Ferme des chutes in Saint-Félicien, QC.

*On a wet fall day or cold wintry night, this hearty traditional fare with a
contemporary flair will comfort all those gathered at your table.*

2	large Yukon Gold potatoes (unpeeled), sliced
2	Tbsp (30 mL) unsalted butter
4	pork and herb sausages
½	white onion, diced
3	cloves garlic, crushed
1	+ ⅔ cups (400 mL) white wine
⅔	cup (150 mL) vegetable stock
2	Tbsp (30 mL) chopped fresh sage
1	+ ½ cups (375 mL) cauliflower florets
2	Tbsp (30 mL) cornstarch
¼	cup (60 mL) water
•	kosher salt and freshly ground black pepper, to taste
1	cup (250 mL) shredded La Chute Chaudière Cheddar

TONY'S SUGGESTIONS
- **DRY WHITE WINE**
  *Riesling from Ontario or
  German Kabinett style Alsace
  Pinot Gris*
- **MEDIUM-BODIED RED WINE**
  Pinot Noir, Beaujolais, Chianti
- **BEER**
  Double Bock

MAKE AHEAD
- *The potatoes and sausage
  mixture can be prepared 1
  day ahead and kept separate,
  covered, and refrigerated.
  Return to room temperature
  before finishing the dish.*

GURTH'S NOTES
- *Use Ivanhoe's Old Sharp Cold
  Pack cheese, or your favourite
  local aged cheddar.*

Cooking Instructions

1 **PREHEAT** the oven to 375°F (190°C) and place the oven rack in the centre position.

2 **FILL** a saucepan with cold water, add the potatoes, and bring to a boil. Cook for 10 minutes until just firm. Set aside.

3 **MELT** the butter in a skillet over medium heat and brown the sausages on all sides, about 8 minutes. Remove the sausages and cut them into thick slices.

4 **ADD** the onions to the same skillet, and cook over medium-low heat for 5 minutes, or until tender. Add the garlic and cook for 1 minute.

5 **ADD** the wine, increase the heat to medium, and cook until the wine has reduced by half.

6 **ADD** the stock, sage, cauliflower, and sausage slices.

7 **IN A MEASURING CUP,** mix the cornstarch with the water until smooth. Stir into the mixture and bring to a boil. Continue to stir as the mixture thickens.

8 **SEASON** with salt and pepper and ladle the mixture into a deep pie plate.

9 **LAYER** the potato slices on top of the sausage mixture.

10 **SPRINKLE** the grated cheese over the potatoes.

11 **BAKE** in the preheated oven for 25 to 30 minutes, or until the cheese is golden.

12 **SERVE** hot.

Lamb Racks in a Puff Blanket
with Les Caprices des saisons

Using Les Caprices des saisons, produced by Fromagerie La Germaine in Saint-Edwidge-de-Clifton, QC.

I love lamb cooked medium-rare. I also prefer buying locally raised lamb. We enjoy the milder flavour and knowing that we are supporting our local sheep industry. Next time you're visiting Vancouver or Victoria, try to sample the famous lamb raised on Salt Spring Island.

1	Tbsp (15 mL) extra virgin olive oil
2	shallots, diced
4	cloves garlic, minced
⅓	cup (75 mL) diced carrot
⅓	cup (75 mL) diced zucchini
1	Tbsp (15 mL) unsalted butter
1	rack of lamb, with 4 chops, cut as 2 portions, bones Frenched
3	oz (75 g) Les Caprices des saisons, rind removed
2	sheets frozen puff pastry, thawed
1	egg, beaten with 1 Tbsp (15 mL) water

FOR THE SAUCE

1	Tbsp (15 mL) unsalted butter
½	carrot, finely diced
¼	onion, finely diced
1	Tbsp (15 mL) brown sugar
1	clove garlic, crushed
2	sprigs fresh thyme, leaves chopped
½	cup (125 mL) sherry
1	cup (250 mL) dry red wine
1	beef bouillon cube dissolved in 1 cup (250 mL) hot water

Cooking instructions continued on following page . . .

TONY'S SUGGESTIONS
- **MEDIUM- TO FULL-BODIED DRY RED WINE**
  Red Bordeaux, Cabernet Sauvignon blends from Ontario or BC, Barolo, Rioja red, Syrah from the northern Rhône
- **FORTIFIED WINE**
  Dry Oloroso sherry
- **BEER**
  Brown ale, Guinness

MAKE AHEAD
- *Cook the diced vegetables for the lamb and sauce a day ahead, cover, and refrigerate.*

GURTH'S NOTES
- *Use other soft, bloomy rind cheese, such as brie, Camembert, Goat Brie, Le Noble, Le Corsaire, or Fleurmier.*
- *This is a dish to prepare when you have plenty of time and want to impress a very special guest.*
- *To French a bone means all the meat has been removed, exposing the bone of a chop or rib. Ask your local butcher if they will do this for you.*

Lamb Racks in a Puff Blanket with Les Caprices des saisons (continued)
Cooking Instructions

1   **PREHEAT** the oven to 425°F (220°C) and place the oven rack in the centre position. Line a baking sheet with parchment paper.

2   **FOR THE LAMB,** heat the oil in a skillet over medium-low temperature. Add the shallots, cover, and cook for 3 minutes.

3   **ADD** the garlic and cook for 1 minute.

4   **STIR** in the carrots and cook for 3 minutes. Add the zucchini and cook for an additional 2 minutes.

5   **REMOVE** the skillet from the heat and let the vegetables cool.

6   **IN A SKILLET,** melt the butter over medium-high heat. Sear the 2 racks on each side for 2 minutes. Remove from the heat and let cool to room temperature.

7   **WITH A KNIFE,** create a hole in the meat section of each portion. Stuff the hole with the cheese.

8   **COAT** each portion with the reserved diced vegetables.

9   **DEPENDING ON THE PUFF PASTRY** you bought, roll or cut the puff pastry so it will be long enough to wrap around the 2 pieces of lamb.

10   **WRAP** the strips of puff pastry around the 2 portions. Brush with the egg mixture to seal the edges. Brush both wrapped racks with the egg wash.

11   **PLACE** the racks on the prepared baking sheet and roast in the preheated oven for 15 to 20 minutes, or until the dough is puffed up and golden.

12   **REMOVE** from the oven, cover loosely with foil, and let rest for 15 minutes.

13   **FOR THE SAUCE,** melt the butter in a small saucepan over medium-low heat. Add the carrot, onion, and sugar. Cook for 5 to 7 minutes.

14   **STIR** in the garlic and thyme; cook for 1 minute.

15   **POUR** in the sherry and wine and heat for 1 minute.

16   **USING** a barbecue lighter, ignite the liquid. It should flambée a little.

17   **ADD** the dissolved beef cube to the saucepan and cook for 15 minutes, reducing the volume by half.

18   **STRAIN** the sauce and keep warm.

19   **TO SERVE,** cut the racks in half, exposing the cheese in the centre of the lamb.

20   **DRIZZLE** the sherry sauce over the exposed meat. Serve over a bed of mixed cooked wild rice and mashed potatoes with your favourite seasonal vegetables.

St. Lawrence Seafood Fondue

Using Pied-de-vent, produced by Fromagerie du Pied-de-Vent in Havre-aux-Maisons, QC; and Le Corsaire, produced by Entreprise de la Ferme Chimo in Douglastown, QC.

Many years ago I prepared a fondue Normande as my Christmas gift to my family. I discovered the recipe in Larousse Gastronomique, a culinary encyclopedia. It was a very rich and decadent dish with Camembert, Livarot, and Pont l'Évèque cheese, shallots, and Calvados, an apple brandy. My dad and I shopped at Montreal Waldman's fishmonger for the seafood. Here is my take on this recipe, using seafood harvested from the Gulf of St. Lawrence, and cheese made in the nearby seaside regions of the Magdalen Islands and the Gaspé.

¾	cup (175 mL) sparkling wine
2	shallots, finely diced
1	Tbsp (15 mL) cornstarch
8	oz (200 g) Pied-de-vent, rind removed, cubed
12	oz (300 g) Le Corsaire, rind removed, cubed
1	+ ½ lb (750 g) cooked, peeled, and deveined medium-sized shrimp
1	lb (500 g) cooked lobster pieces
1	baguette, cubed

Cooking Instructions

1   **IN A LARGE SAUCEPAN,** combine ½ cup (125 mL) of the sparkling wine and the shallots; simmer for 5 minutes.

2   **IN A MEASURING CUP,** mix the remaining ¼ cup (60 mL) sparkling wine with the cornstarch, stirring until smooth.

3   **ADDING** a little at a time, stir both cheeses into the wine/shallot mixture.

4   **WHEN ALL THE CHEESE HAS MELTED,** whisk in the cornstarch mixture and cook for 3 to 5 minutes, or until thickened.

5   **TRANSFER** the melted cheese mixture to the fondue pot. Set the pot on the fondue stand over the heat source.

6   **ARRANGE** the shrimp, lobster, and bread cubes on a platter and supply long forks for dipping. Dip away!

TONY'S SUGGESTIONS
- **DRY WHITE WINE**
  Chablis, unoaked Chardonnay, Pinot Blanc, Pinot Grigio
- **DRY ROSÉ**
  Tavel or Bandol
- **DRY SPARKLING WINE**
  Prosecco, Spanish cava, Ontario or BC sparkling
- **FORTIFIED WINE**
  Fino or Manzanilla sherry (chilled)
- **BEER**
  Czech Pilsner, German Kolsch, Bavarian Weiss
- **SPIRITS**
  Ice-cold vodka

MAKE AHEAD
- *Cheese can be cut 1 day ahead, covered, and refrigerated.*

GURTH'S NOTES
- *Use your favourite soft, bloomy rind cheese, such as brie, and your favourite semi-soft washed rind cheese, such as Oka Providence, instead.*
- *Try using other cooked seafood, such as crab or scallops.*

Chicken Galantine
with Piacere & Toasted Pecans

Using Piacere, produced by Monforte Dairy Company Ltd. in Millbank, ON.

A galantine is a classic French dish where the meat has been boned and stuffed. The meat is rolled in plastic wrap or cheesecloth and poached in stock. It is traditionally chilled and glazed with aspic prior to serving. This is where my version differs, for it is served hot with accompanying condiments.

2	Tbsp (30 mL) extra virgin olive oil
1	shallot, finely diced
1	cup (250 mL) boiling water
½	cup (125 mL) couscous
2	Tbsp (30 mL) toasted and chopped pecans
3	oz (75 g) Piacere cheese, crumbled
2	chicken breasts
4	cups (1 L) chicken stock

Cooking instructions continued on following page . . .

TONY'S SUGGESTIONS
- FULL-BODIED, DRY, OAK-AGED WHITE WINE
California or Australian Chardonnay, white Burgundy, Ontario Chardonnay, BC Pinot Gris, Alsace Pinot Gris
- BEER
Lager

MAKE AHEAD
- *Galantine can be prepared to the poaching stage a day ahead, covered, and refrigerated.*

GURTH'S NOTES
- *Piacere is a tangy cheese with herbs and spices on the rind. You can substitute Borgonzola or a soft, bloomy rind cheese such as Les Caprices des saisons, Le Cendré des prés, brie, or Bouq' Émissaire.*

Chicken Galantine with Piacere & Toasted Pecans *(continued)*
Cooking Instructions

1 **IN A SMALL SKILLET,** heat 1 Tbsp (15 mL) of the oil over medium-low temperature. Cook the shallots for 3 minutes, or until soft. Set aside.

2 **IN A BOWL,** combine the boiling water and couscous. Cover with plastic wrap and set aside for 5 minutes, or until all the water has been absorbed.

3 **MIX** in the cooked shallots, pecans, and cheese.

4 **WORKING** with 1 at a time, place a chicken breast between 2 layers of plastic wrap and gently flatten with a mallet until it's a uniform 1/8 inch (3 mm) thick.

5 **PLACE** 1/4 of the couscous-cheese mixture at the wide end of the flattened breast.

6 **ROLL** the chicken into a tight roll, using the plastic wrap to make it as tight as possible.

7 **MAKE** sure the plastic completely encloses the roll and twist the ends to seal it completely. Repeat this process to stuff the other chicken breasts.

8 **IN A LARGE SAUCEPAN,** bring the chicken stock to a boil.

9 **PLACE** the wrapped chicken rolls in the broth, lower the heat to a simmer, and cover. Poach the galantine for approximately 10 to 20 minutes, depending on their size.

10 **REMOVE** the plastic wrap from the galantine. Slice each rolled breast into 4 to 5 pieces. Place the pieces on the plate leaning on each other slightly.

11 **SERVE** with steamed Brussels sprouts and peas, green onions, and a spoonful of Dijon mustard.

Crab-Stuffed Chicken Breasts
with Herb & Garlic Gouda Sauce

Using Herb and Garlic Gouda, produced by Cheeselady's Gouda Cheese in Winsloe North, PEI.

Chicken can be used in so many different ways: breaded and fried, roasted, poached, grilled, or Indian butter chicken, chicken tika, cordon bleu, à la king … this version stuffs chicken breasts with crabmeat and cooks them in a Gouda sauce.

1	Tbsp (15 mL) extra virgin olive oil
½	red onion, diced
¼	red bell pepper, diced
1	stalk celery, diced
4	oz (100 g) cooked crabmeat
1	Tbsp (15 mL) chopped fresh dill
2	Tbsp (30 mL) lemon juice
•	kosher salt and freshly ground black pepper, to taste
4	boneless, skinless chicken breasts
3	Tbsp (45 mL) unsalted butter
3	Tbsp (45 mL) all-purpose flour
2	cups (500 mL) cold milk
1	cup (250 mL) grated Herb and Garlic Gouda
•	fresh dill sprigs, for garnish

Cooking instructions continued on following page …

TONY'S SUGGESTIONS
- **DRY WHITE WINE**
  White Burgundy, unoaked Chardonnay, Grüner Veltliner, Soave, Pinot Gris
- **FORTIFIED WINE**
  Fino or Manzanilla sherry
- **BEER**
  Belgian Saison, pale ale

MAKE AHEAD
- *Chicken breasts can be flattened and filled 1 day ahead, covered, and refrigerated. Bring to room temperature prior to roasting.*

GURTH'S NOTES
- *Use flavoured cheddar, Monterey Jack, havarti, or mozzarella instead of Gouda.*
- *Stuff with chopped cooked shrimp, lobster, or scallops.*

Crab-Stuffed Chicken Breasts with Herb & Garlic Gouda Sauce (continued)
Cooking Instructions

1   **PREHEAT** the oven to 350°F (180°C) and place the oven rack in the centre position. Spray an 8-inch (2-L) square baking dish with cooking oil.

2   **IN A SMALL SKILLET,** heat the oil over medium-low temperature. Add the onion and cook for 3 to 4 minutes, or until tender.

3   **ADD** the red pepper and celery and cook for 3 minutes, or until soft and tender. Remove from the heat and let cool.

4   **ADD** the crabmeat, dill, and lemon juice to the mixture. Season with salt and pepper. Set aside.

5   **WORKING WITH ONE AT A TIME,** place a chicken breast between 2 layers of plastic wrap and use a mallet to gently flatten it to 1/8 inch (3 mm) thick.

6   **SPOON** 1/4 of the crab mixture onto the narrow end of the chicken breast and roll it up tightly. Repeat with the remaining chicken breasts and crab mixture.

7   **PLACE** the stuffed chicken breasts in the greased casserole dish. Place in the preheated oven and roast for 10 to 12 minutes.

8   **IN A SMALL SAUCEPAN,** melt the butter over medium temperature. Add the flour and stir and cook for 3 minutes.

9   **SLOWLY** drizzle the cold milk into the mixture, whisking continually to prevent lumps from forming. Cook for 5 to 7 minutes, until thickened.

10 **ADD** the cheese and stir until melted.

11 **POUR** the sauce over the chicken breasts and return to the oven for 10 minutes, or until golden.

12 **COOL** for a few minutes before serving. Garnish each serving with a sprig of dill.

Papillotes of Sole
with Mediterranean Stuffing

Using Feta cheese, produced by Ewenity Dairy Co-operative in Conn, ON.

Cooking fillets of fish inside paper is easy and tasty. Best of all, the fish will not dry out from being overcooked. It cooks in its own steam.

2	Tbsp (30 mL) extra virgin olive oil
1	small red onion, chopped
2	cloves garlic, chopped
½	cup (125 mL) diced fennel
8	sun-dried tomatoes, soaked in warm water and sliced
1	Tbsp (15 mL) chopped fresh oregano
⅓	cup (75 mL) pitted and chopped black olives
3	oz (75 g) Ewenity Feta cheese, crumbled
•	kosher salt and freshly ground black pepper, to taste
4	sole fillets

TONY'S SUGGESTIONS
- **CRISP, DRY WHITE WINE**
  Muscadet, Soave, Chablis, unoaked Ontario or BC Chardonnay
- **ROSÉ**
  chilled
- **SPARKLING WINE**
  Brut
- **FORTIFIED WINE**
  Fino sherry (chilled)
- **BEER** *Pilsner*

MAKE AHEAD
- *The filling can be made 1 day ahead, covered, and refrigerated.*

GURTH'S NOTES
- *Try using a soft chèvre for this recipe.*
- *Use rinsed capers instead of olives.*
- *Experiment by using different fresh fish, such as salmon, arctic char, or pickerel.*

Cooking Instructions

1 **PREHEAT** the oven to 350°F (180°C) and place the oven rack in the centre position.

2 **IN A SMALL SKILLET,** heat 1 Tbsp (15 mL) of the oil over medium-low temperature. Add the onions and cook for approximately 5 minutes.

3 **ADD** the garlic and cook for 1 minute.

4 **ADD** the fennel and cook for 5 minutes.

5 **REMOVE** the skillet from the heat and let cool.

6 **ADD** the tomatoes, oregano, olives, and cheese. Season with salt and pepper.

7 **USING A VERY SHARP,** thin filleting knife, cut down along the centre ridge of the fillet, halfway through the piece of fish. Once this incision is done with the knife still in the fish, cut and turn the knife's blade towards the right edge. Carefully slice up to 1/3 inch (8 mm) from the edge. This cut creates a flap on one side of the fish.

8 **REPEAT** the cut from the centre to the left edge. Open both the right and left flaps.

9 **FILL** each opening with the onion and cheese mixture and fold the flaps over the filling.

10 **CUT** 4 large pieces of parchment paper into heart shapes. Brush with olive oil and fold in half lengthwise.

11 **PLACE** each fillet close to the fold. Fold the parchment paper over the fish.

12 **BEGINNING AT THE POINTED END,** fold the edges together to seal the sole inside.

13 **PLACE** on a baking sheet and bake for 10 to 15 minutes.

14 **SERVE** the paper packages on individual plates. Your guests will enjoy the aroma as soon as they cut open their papillotes.

Duck Breast in Cognac
with Grizzly Rösti

Using Grizzly Gouda, produced by Sylvan Star Cheese Ltd. in Sylvan Lake, AB.

When Joanne and I travelled to Quebec several years ago to research The Definitive Guide to Canadian Artisanal and Fine Cheese, *we dined at many restaurants. Joanne became a fan of duck breast. She found it so juicy and tasty. During the 1996 Atlanta Olympics, I worked at a resort and spa just north of the city. My executive chef was Austrian. Along with the other line cooks, I prepared many Austrian/German/Swiss dishes such as rösti. You can prepare rösti from cooled, cooked potatoes; though it doesn't take as long to cook, I find the texture isn't as crispy. Try it both ways and you be the judge. This recipe is a marriage of both experiences, which Joanne enjoys every time I prepare it for her.*

1	duck breast, cut in a criss-cross pattern
¼	cup (60 mL) cognac
1	shallot, finely diced
3	garlic cloves, minced
2	baking potatoes, peeled, grated, and squeezed dry
2	oz (50 g) Grizzly Gouda, grated
1	+ ½ tsp (7.5 mL) whole caraway seeds
2	Tbsp (30 mL) unsalted butter
2	Tbsp (30 mL) duck fat

Cooking instructions continued on following page . . .

TONY'S SUGGESTIONS
- **MEDIUM- TO FULL-BODIED DRY RED WINE**
  Oregon or New Zealand Pinot Noir, red Burgundy, California Merlot, Ontario or BC Meritage Riesling, Gewurztraminer
- **FORTIFIED WINE**
  Dry Oloroso sherry
- **BEER**
  Pale ale, Trappist ale

MAKE AHEAD
- *Potatoes can be grated 2 days ahead, stored in water, covered, and refrigerated. Squeeze them dry prior to using.*

GURTH'S NOTES
- *Duck breast tastes best when cooked medium-rare, 125°F (52°C). Vary the cooking times according to the thickness and size of the breast you're cooking.*
- *Dry, hard cheese, such as Montasio, Parmesan, old Gouda, or Grano Padano, would be tasty substitutes.*

Duck Breast in Cognac with Grizzly Rösti *(continued)*
Cooking Instructions

1 **HEAT** a skillet to medium-high. Place the duck skin-side down and cook for 10 minutes, or until the skin is very crispy and golden-brown.

2 **FLIP** the breast over and cook the other side for 5 to 7 minutes. Transfer to a plate, cover loosely with foil, and let the meat rest for 15 minutes. Reserve 2 Tbsp (30 mL) of the fat and discard the rest.

3 **ADD** the cognac to the hot skillet and stir with a wooden spoon. Cook until the volume has reduced by half. Keep warm.

4 **IN A BOWL,** combine the shallot, garlic, potatoes, cheese, and caraway seeds.

5 **IN A LARGE SKILLET,** melt the butter over medium temperature. Add the reserved duck fat.

6 **SPOON** the potato/cheese mixture into the skillet, covering the entire surface and pressing the potatoes down lightly.

7 **COOK** for 10 to 12 minutes, or until golden on the bottom.

8 **PLACE** a large plate upside-down over the skillet. Turn the skillet over so the rösti falls onto the plate.

9 **SLIDE** the rösti back into the skillet, so the cooked side is up. Cook for 5 to 10 minutes, or until golden on the bottom.

10 **CUT** the rösti in quarters and place each quarter on a serving plate.

11 **CUT** thin slices from the duck breast and place them on the plates in a fan-like arrangement beside the rösti.

12 **DRIZZLE** the warm cognac sauce over the duck breast and serve with your favourite vegetables.

Pheasant Gratinée
with Le Moine Cheese

Using Le Moine cheese, produced by Abbaye de Saint-Benoît-du-Lac in Saint-Benoît-du-Lac, QC.

When my family lived in Ottawa, my Dad gave his business clients locally raised pheasants as Christmas gifts one year. Of course he ordered a few extra birds for my family and I to enjoy. Pheasant is a very lean meat and requires extra fat—in this case the 35% cream and cheese—to ensure it doesn't dry out while cooking. The cheese and Dijon sauce give the pheasant great flavour.

2	Tbsp (30 mL) unsalted butter
1	pheasant, cut into 8 pieces
•	kosher salt and freshly ground white pepper, to taste
2	shallots, diced
3	cloves of garlic, minced
½	cup (125 mL) white wine
1	cup (250 mL) 35% cream
1	Tbsp (15 mL) Dijon mustard
4	oz (100 g) Le Moine, shredded
•	pinch of cayenne
½	cup (125 mL) panko or fresh breadcrumbs

Cooking instructions continued on following page . . .

TONY'S SUGGESTIONS
- **MEDIUM-BODIED, DRY RED WINE**
  Red Burgundy, Ontario or BC Pinot Noir, Barbaresco, Chianti Classico Riserva, Super Tuscan reds
- **OLD WORLD WHITE WINE**
  Burgundy, Blanc de Blancs champagne
- **BEER**
  Doppelbock, Porter, Dark Lager

GURTH'S NOTES
- *If pheasant is unavailable, use guinea fowl or chicken.*
- *Your favourite local Swiss, Gruyère, or Emmenthal cheese can be used.*

Pheasant Gratinée with Le Moine Cheese *(continued)*
Cooking Instructions

1 **PREHEAT** the oven to 350°F (180°C) and place the oven rack in the centre position.

2 **IN A LARGE SAUCEPAN,** melt the butter over medium heat. Sprinkle the pheasant pieces with salt and pepper, and place in the saucepan. Cook covered, for 5 minutes.

3 **TRANSFER** to a large ovenproof dish and set aside.

4 **ADD** the shallots and garlic to the saucepan, and cook over medium heat for 2 minutes.

5 **POUR** in the wine. Increase the heat to maximum and cook until the wine has reduced by half.

6 **REDUCE** the heat to medium-low and pour in the cream.

7 **STIR** in the mustard and ½ of the cheese; cook for 5 minutes, or until thickened.

8 **STIR** in the cayenne.

9 **POUR** the sauce over the pheasant. Sprinkle the panko and the remaining cheese overtop.

10 **PLACE** the pheasant in the oven and roast for 20 minutes, or until the cheese is golden.

Stuffed Turkey Thighs
with Aged Pepato

Using Aged Pepato, produced by International Cheese in Toronto, ON.

I tested this recipe on my unsuspecting parents. I didn't tell them I was creating recipes for a new book, and at the end of the meal, I asked if it was tasty enough to be in a cookbook. They loudly voiced their affirmation. I informed them they'd unknowingly joined my Guinea Pig Club of recipe tasters. Anytime I needed their taste buds, "Call us!" was their response. Roasted vegetables and garlic-mashed potatoes are delicious accompaniments.

4	skinless, boneless turkey thighs
1	Tbsp (15 mL) extra virgin olive oil
½	large red onion, diced
•	kosher salt and freshly ground black pepper, to taste
4	Swiss chard leaves, stemmed
7	oz (175 g) Aged Pepato cheese
2	Tbsp (30 mL) unsalted butter

TONY'S SUGGESTIONS

- **FULL-BODIED, DRY WHITE WINE**
  New World Chardonnay, New Zealand Sauvignon Blanc
- **FRUIT-DRIVEN RED WINE**
  Ontario or BC Pinot Noir, named village Beaujolais (Morgon, Fleurie, St. Amour, etc.)
- **SPARKLING WINE**
  Shiraz
- **BEER**
  Lager
- **SPARKLING CIDER**

MAKE AHEAD

- *Turkey thighs can be stuffed and rolled a day ahead, covered, and refrigerated. Bring to room temperature before roasting.*

GURTH'S NOTES

- *Try using Gouda, havarti, Peperonato, Valbert, or Swiss.*

Cooking Instructions

1 **PREHEAT** the oven to 375°F (190°C) and place the oven rack in the centre position.

2 **WORKING** with 1 at a time, place the turkey thighs between 2 layers of plastic wrap and use a mallet to flatten them to ⅛ inch (3 mm) thick.

3 **IN A SKILLET** over medium-low temperature, heat the oil and add the onions; cover and cook until tender, approximately 5 minutes. Remove the skillet from the heat and set aside.

4 **SPRINKLE** salt and pepper on the inside flesh of each thigh.

5 **BRING** a saucepan of water to a simmer and blanch each Swiss chard leaf for 3 seconds. Immerse immediately in ice water to cool and pat dry.

6 **COVER** each thigh with the cooked onions.

7 **PLACE** a Swiss chard leaf over the onions.

8 **CUT** four 1-oz (25-g) chunks of cheese from the block. Cut the remaining cheese into 4 slices.

9 **PLACE** the cheese chunks on top of the Swiss chard. Roll up each thigh and tie it with butcher's twine.

10 **IN A LARGE OVENPROOF SKILLET,** melt the butter over medium-high heat.

11 **SEAR** the turkey rolls until golden on all sides, approximately 4 to 5 minutes.

12 **PLACE** a cheese slice on top of each thigh and place the skillet in the oven.

13 **ROAST** for 7 to 10 minutes, until the cheese is melted and the turkey is cooked through and a meat thermometer inserted into the thickest part registers 165°F (74°C).

14 **TRANSFER** the thighs to a plate, cover, and let rest for 10 minutes.

15 **TO SERVE,** remove the string, cut the rolls in half diagonally, and cross one over the other on the plate.

Smoked Salmon
with Sainte-Martine Pasta Sauce

Using Sainte-Martine, produced by Fromagerie de l'Alpage in Châteauguay, QC.

This dish received two thumbs up from Joanne—one for the taste of smoked salmon and the other for its beneficial omega-3 essential fatty acids. These EFAs are good for your cardiovascular health and help lower blood pressure.

1	leek, white parts only, rinsed
3	Tbsp (45 mL) unsalted butter
3	Tbsp (45 mL) all-purpose flour
2	cups (500 mL) milk
3	oz (75 g) Sainte-Martine cheese, sliced, rind removed
⅔	cup (75 mL) packed, sliced arugula
¼	cup (60 mL) chopped fresh dill
1	Tbsp (15 mL) fresh lemon juice
•	kosher salt and freshly ground black pepper, to taste
4	cups (1 L) cooked rotini pasta, warm
6	smoked salmon slices, cut into thin strips

Cooking Instructions

1 **CUT** the leek in half lengthwise. Cut thin half-moon slices.
2 **IN A SAUCEPAN,** melt the butter over medium-low heat. Add the leeks, cover, and cook for 3 to 5 minutes, or until tender.
3 **STIR** in the flour and cook for 3 minutes.
4 **SLOWLY** drizzle in the milk, whisking to ensure no lumps form. Cook for 7 to 10 minutes, or until the sauce thickens slightly.
5 **ADD** the cheese and stir until it melts.
6 **STIR** in the arugula, dill, and lemon juice. Season with salt and pepper.
7 **IN A LARGE BOWL,** combine the warm pasta with the sauce. Toss to coat well.
8 **DIVIDE** amongst individual pasta bowls and garnish with the smoked salmon.

TONY'S SUGGESTIONS
- **AROMATIC, DRY WHITE WINE**
  Gewuztraminer, dry Riesling, Alsace Muscat
- **SPARKLING WINE**
  Brut
- **FORTIFIED WINE**
  Fino or Manzanilla sherry
- **BEER**
  Lager, pale pilsner, smoked beer

MAKE AHEAD
- *Sauce can be made ahead a day ahead, cooled, covered, and refrigerated. Reheat prior to serving.*

GURTH'S NOTES
- *Use brie, Camembert, Le Noble, Le Corsaire, or other similar soft, bloomy rind cheese.*

Onion & Mushroom Perogies

Using Konig Strasse, a German butter cheese, produced by The Village Cheese Co. in Armstrong, BC.

This is a dish to make in large quantities and freeze for future enjoyment. Have a perogy party and invite friends over to help make and assemble the filled pockets of dough. At the end of the day, everyone leaves with a tray or bag of perogies.

2	cups (500 mL) all-purpose flour
½	tsp (2 mL) salt
1	egg, beaten
1	Tbsp (15 mL) canola oil
½	cup (125 mL) hot water
4	Tbsp (60 mL) unsalted butter
1	onion, finely diced
4	portobello mushrooms, gills removed, flesh diced
4	oz (100 g) Konig Strasse cheese, shredded
•	kosher salt and freshly ground black pepper, to taste
1	egg, beaten with 1 Tbsp (15 mL) water
•	caramelized onions, sour cream, and chives, for garnish

TONY'S SUGGESTIONS
- MEDIUM-BODIED, DRY WHITE WINE
  Alsace Riesling or Pinot Gris or Pinot Blanc, Ontario Riesling, dry
- RED WINE
  Pinot Noir or Beaujolais-Villages at room temperature, Barolo, Chianti
- SPARKLING WINE
  dry
- FORTIFIED WINE
  Palo Cortado sherry, Sercial (Madeira)
- BEER
  Brown Ale

MAKE AHEAD
- *Prepare up to a month ahead and freeze individually on a baking sheet lined with waxed paper. When frozen, place in a freezer bag.*
- *Cook in boiling water from a frozen state for 8 minutes.*

GURTH'S NOTES
- *Use another mild cheese, such as cheddar, havarti, Edam, Esrom, or Munster*

Cooking Instructions

1   **IN A LARGE BOWL,** combine the flour and salt. Make a well in the centre of the mixture.

2   **IN A MEASURING CUP,** mix the egg and oil together; pour into the centre of the well and stir.

3   **POUR** in the water and stir until the dough clumps together in a ball.

4   **ON A LIGHTLY FLOURED SURFACE,** knead the dough until it becomes soft and silky, approximately 5 to 7 minutes.

5   **COVER** with plastic wrap and let rest for 30 minutes.

6   **IN A SKILLET,** melt 1 Tbsp (15 mL) of the butter over medium-low heat. Add the onion, cover, and cook for 5 to 7 minutes, or until tender.

7   **STIR** in the diced mushroom and cook for another 3 to 5 minutes. Remove the skillet from the heat and let cool to room temperature.

8   **ADD** the shredded cheese to the cooled onion/mushroom mixture. Season with salt and pepper.

9   **ON A LIGHTLY FLOURED SURFACE,** roll the dough to $1/8$-inch (3-mm) thickness.

10 **USING** a floured 3-inch (8-cm) biscuit cutter or large water glass, cut the dough into circles.

11 **BRUSH** the edge of each circle with the egg/water mixture.

12 **PLACE** a heaping tablespoon of the onion/cheese mixture in the centre of each circle.

13 **FOLD** the dough over and press down along the edges, creating a tight seal.

14 **FORM** the scraps of dough into a ball, roll out, cut more circles, and fill as above. Continue until all the dough or filling is used.

15 **BRING** a large pot of salted water to a boil. Line a baking sheet with waxed paper.

16 **WORKING** in batches, boil the perogies. When they float at the surface, approximately 3 to 5 minutes, transfer them to the baking sheet with a slotted spoon.

17 **IN A LARGE SKILLET,** melt 1 Tbsp (15 mL) of the butter over medium-high heat. Pan-fry $1/3$ of the boiled perogies until golden on both sides. Repeat with the remaining butter and perogies.

18 **SERVE** on a platter, garnished with caramelized onions and chives, with a bowl of sour cream on the side.

Spinach, Mascarpone & Quark-Filled Salmon Fillets

Using Mascarpone, produced by Saputo Inc. in Saint-Léonard, QC; Parmesan, producedo by Fromagerie Saint-Laurent in Saint-Bruno, QC; and Quark, produced by Fox Hill Cheese House in Port Williams, NS.

This recipe was a crowd pleaser when Joanne and I served it to friends at a dinner party. The crusty top hid the creamy filling inside the salmon. No sauce is required for this dish, making it even easier to prepare. Serve with Israeli couscous, steamed local asparagus, baby carrots, and pattypan squash.

5	oz (125 g) fresh baby spinach leaves
¼	cup (60 mL) Fox Hill Cheese House Quark, at room temperature
¼	cup (60 mL) Saputo Mascarpone, at room temperature
•	pinch ground nutmeg
4	salmon fillets (about 6 oz/150 g each)
2	cups (500 mL) panko or fresh white breadcrumbs
¼	cup (60 mL) unsalted butter, melted
½	cup (125 mL) freshly grated Fromagerie Saint-Laurent Parmesan

Cooking instructions continued on following page . . .

TONY'S SUGGESTIONS
- **DRY WHITE WINE**
  Burgundy, Ontario or BC Chardonnay or Pinot Gris, Sauvignon Blanc
- **RED WINE**
  Ontario/BC Pinot Noir, red Burgundy, or Beaujolais
- **BEER**
  Saison

MAKE AHEAD
- *Stuff the salmon up to 1 day ahead, cover, and refrigerate. Return to room temperature prior to roasting.*

GURTH'S NOTES
- *Substitute cream cheese if quark is unavailable. Try Swiss chard or beet greens in place of spinach.*

Spinach, Mascarpone, & Quark-Filled Salmon Fillets (continued)
Cooking Instructions

1 **PREHEAT** the oven to 350°F (180°C) and place the oven rack in the centre position. Spray a baking sheet with cooking oil.

2 **PLACE** a small saucepan over medium-low heat, add the spinach, and cook covered until wilted, approximately 2 to 3 minutes. No water is required for the spinach leaves, which contain lots of moisture.

3 **DRAIN** the spinach and allow to cool.

4 **WHEN COOL ENOUGH TO HANDLE,** squeeze to remove as much liquid as possible.

5 **PLACE** in a food processor and pulse until finely chopped. Add the quark, mascarpone, and nutmeg and process until smooth. Set aside.

6 **MAKE** a cut in each salmon fillet, creating a pocket opening. From the top, beginning ½ inch (1 cm) from the end, make a ¾-inch-deep (2-cm) cut, ending ½ inch (1 cm) from the opposite end.

7 **DIVIDE** the spinach/cheese mixture into 4 portions and stuff each fillet.

8 **IN A SMALL BOWL,** combine the panko, butter, and Parmesan. Coat the top of each fillet with the mixture.

9 **PLACE** the salmon fillets on the prepared baking sheet and roast for 10 to 15 minutes, or until the centre is warmed through.

Raclette of Beer-Washed Cheese
with Grilled Scallops & Vegetables

Using L' Héritage with Trois-Pistoles, produced by Fromagerie des Basques in Trois-Pistoles, QC; Raclette Griffon, produced by Fromagerie Kaiser in Noyan, QC; and La Barre du Jour, produced by Fromagerie Le P'tit Train du Nord Inc. in Mont-Laurier, QC.

Raclette is both a type of cheese and a machine to melt it—another great innovation by the Swiss, well known for their fondue. The raclette machine is a wonderful and entertaining party accessory. You invite your guests to heat or grill their food and melt the cheese of their choice. I use mine at cocktail parties and dinners. It's always popular with my friends.

1	lb (500 g) baby potatoes, halved
1	tsp (5 mL) kosher salt
1	cauliflower, cut into florets
1	stalk broccoli, cut into florets
4	oz (100 g) L' Héritage cheese, sliced
4	oz (100 g) Raclette Griffon cheese, sliced
4	oz (100 g) La Barre du Jour cheese, sliced
1	+ ½ lb (750 g) fresh, deep sea scallops
1	baguette, sliced

Cooking instructions continued on following page . . .

TONY'S SUGGESTIONS
- **MEDIUM-BODIED, DRY WHITE WINE**
  Sauvignon Blanc from the Loire, New Zealand or Ontario or BC, dry Riesling
- **LIGHT-BODIED, DRY RED**
  Chilled Beaujolais or Ontario or BC Gamay
- **SPARKLING WINE**
  Prosecco or Spanish cava
- **FORTIFIED WINE**
  Chilled dry sherry
- **BEER**
  Pale ale
- **SPIRITS**
  Ice-cold vodka

MAKE AHEAD
- *Potatoes, cauliflower, and broccoli can be blanched as much as 1 day ahead, covered, and refrigerated.*

GURTH'S NOTES
- *Use other washed cheese such as Grand Chouffe, Délices des Appalaches, Red Dawn, Cru des érables, or Oka.*

Raclette of Beer-Washed Cheese with Grilled Scallops & Vegetables (continued)
Cooking Instructions

1 **FILL** a large pot with cold water, add the potatoes, and bring to a boil. Cook for 5 to 7 minutes, or until tender.

2 **REMOVE** the potatoes with a slotted spoon and place them in a bowl of ice-cold water.

3 **ADD** the salt and cauliflower to the boiling water and cook for 4 to 5 minutes, or until just tender.

4 **REMOVE** the cauliflower with a slotted spoon and place in a separate bowl of ice-cold water.

5 **REPEAT** with the broccoli, cooking it in the same water.

6 **DRAIN** the vegetables and place in separate serving bowls.

7 **SLICE** the cheese and arrange on a platter.

8 **TURN** the raclette machine to the medium-high setting.

9 **SUPPLY** each guest with a plate and invite them to broil the vegetables and cheese of their choice in the individual raclette pans.

10 **GUESTS COOK THE SCALLOPS** on the hot grill surface above the broiler for 2 to 3 minutes on each side.

11 **THEY CAN POUR** the melted cheese over their grilled scallops, the reheated vegetables, or on a slice of baguette.

12 **LET COOL** briefly and enjoy!

Baked Lobster Pennoni
with Dill Mozzarella Sauce

Using Dill Mozzarella, produced by Empire Cheese and Butter Co-operative in Campbellford, ON.

This has a triple taste of dill: chopped fresh dill is mixed with lobster in the pasta tubes, the cheese contains dill seed, and the garnish is sprigs of dill. For anyone who loves this herb (as Joanne does), the dish is dill-icious! A smart husband cooks recipes with ingredients his wife loves.

2	Tbsp (30 mL) unsalted butter
2	shallots, diced
2	Tbsp (30 mL) all-purpose flour
2	cups (500 mL) milk
7	oz (175 g) Dill Mozzarella, shredded
1	+ ¼ cup (310 mL) cooked and diced lobster
2	Tbsp (30 mL) chopped fresh dill
10	pennoni tubes
•	fresh dill sprigs, for garnish

TONY'S SUGGESTIONS
- **FULL-BODIED, DRY WHITE WINE**
  White Burgundy, California Chardonnay, Ontario or BC barrel-aged Chardonnay, Château Chalon
- **FORTIFIED WINE**
  Palo Cortado, dry Oloroso, Sercial
- **BEER**
  India Pale Ale

MAKE AHEAD
- *Sauce can be made 1 day ahead, covered, and refrigerated.*

GURTH'S NOTES
- *Try a flavoured Gouda or havarti.*
- *Use other cooked seafood, such as shrimp or crab.*
- *Pennoni is a large straight tube that's a little smaller than cannelloni. If you can't find pennoni at your grocery store, use cannelloni; it holds more filling and takes longer to cook.*

Cooking Instructions

1   **PREHEAT** the oven to 350°F (180°C) and place the rack in the centre position. Spray an 11- x 7-inch (2-L) baking dish with cooking oil.

2   **IN A MEDIUM-SIZED SAUCEPAN,** melt the butter over medium heat. Cook the shallots for 3 minutes. Stir in the flour and cook for 2 minutes.

3   **DRIZZLE** the milk into the mixture, whisking constantly to prevent lumps from forming. Cook for 5 minutes, stirring occasionally.

4   **STIR** in the cheese and cook for 3 minutes, or until thickened.

5   **IN A SMALL BOWL,** combine the lobster and chopped dill.

6   **FILL** the pennoni tubes with the lobster mixture, either by hand or using a piping bag.

7   **PLACE** the filled pennoni in the prepared dish. Ladle the cheese sauce over the pasta.

8   **COVER** and bake in the preheated oven for 35 minutes.

9   **REMOVE** from the oven and let sit for 5 minutes prior to serving. Garnish with fresh dill.

PREPARATION TIME 1 HR
COOKING TIME 1 HR
MAKES 6 LARGE SERVINGS

Brown Rice Cheddar Tart
with Roasted Tomatoes & Broccoli

Using Extra-Old Cheddar, produced by Fromagerie L'Ancêtre Inc. in Bécancour, QC, and Le Pampille, produced by Fromagerie Ruban Bleu in Saint Isidore, QC.

Who would have thought you could use cooked rice as a crust? Joanne read about this in a holistic nutrition article and challenged me to develop a recipe using it. She was very pleased with my culinary efforts. When cooking brown rice, rinse it well under cold running water to remove the powdery starch. Bring 1 cup (250 mL) of salted water to a boil in a small pot and add ½ cup (125 mL) of rice. Return to a boil and stir once. Reduce the heat to minimum, cover, and simmer for 50 minutes. Remove the pot from the heat and let stand, covered, for 5 minutes before fluffing with a fork. Yields approximately 1½ cups (375 mL).

TONY'S SUGGESTIONS
- **DRY, FULL-BODIED WHITE WINE**
  white Rhône, white Bordeaux, Pouilly-Fumé, Ontario oak-aged Chardonnay, BC Pinot Gris
- **RED WINE**
  Chianti, Nebbiolo d'Alba, Côtes du Rhône-Villages
- **BEER**
  Brown ale

MAKE AHEAD
- *Crust can be made a day ahead, covered, and refrigerated. Bring to room temperature before finishing the dish.*

GURTH'S NOTES
- *Use your favourite nippy cheddar and locally available soft goat cheese for this recipe.*

FOR THE BROWN RICE CRUST

1	cup (250 mL) cooked medium-grain brown rice
1	cup (250 mL) shredded Extra-Old Cheddar
2	eggs, lightly beaten

FOR THE FILLING

6	Roma tomatoes, halved lengthwise
9	cloves garlic, unpeeled
2	Tbsp (30 mL) extra virgin olive oil
1	+ ½ cups (375 mL) broccoli florets
2	oz (50 g) Le Pampille goat cheese, crumbled
4	eggs, lightly beaten
¼	cup (60 mL) milk
3	green onions, sliced
1	tsp (5 mL) dried tarragon
•	freshly ground black pepper, to taste

Cooking instructions continued on following page . . .

Brown Rice Cheddar Tart with Roasted Tomatoes & Broccoli (continued)
Cooking Instructions

1   **PREHEAT** the oven to 400°F (200°C) and place the oven rack in the centre position. Spray a 10-inch (25-cm) quiche dish with cooking oil.

2   **IN A BOWL,** combine the rice, cheddar cheese, and the 2 beaten eggs, mixing well. Spread the mixture over the base and sides of the prepared dish.

3   **BAKE** for 15 minutes in the preheated oven. Remove from the oven and set aside to cool. Reduce the oven temperature to 350°F (180°C).

4   **COMBINE** the tomatoes, garlic, and oil in a bowl and stir to coat well. Place in a roasting pan and roast for 30 minutes, or until the tomatoes and garlic become soft. Remove the pan from the oven, let cool slightly, and peel the softened garlic.

5   **ARRANGE** the broccoli over the bottom of the rice crust. Top with the tomatoes, garlic, and goat cheese.

6   **IN A BOWL,** stir in the remaining eggs, milk, green onions, tarragon, and pepper; pour over the tomatoes.

7   **PLACE** the dish on a baking sheet and bake for 60 minutes, or until set.

8   **REMOVE** from the oven and let cool for 5 minutes before serving

Sicilian Pasta Timbale

Using Provolone and Romano Salemo, produced by Salerno Dairy in Hamilton, ON.

This is a great dish to serve at the table so your guests can see it before it's cut into portions. What cook does not like receiving a round of applause or hearing the oohs and aahs of appreciation from dinner guests? It feeds the ego and is the reward for the hard work in the kitchen.

FOR THE MARINARA SAUCE

1	tsp (5 mL) extra virgin olive oil
3	cloves garlic, minced
1	28-oz (796-mL) can tomato purée
¼	cup (60 mL) chopped fresh basil
•	kosher salt and freshly ground black pepper, to taste

FOR THE PASTA TIMBALE

3	small eggplants
1	Tbsp (15 mL) kosher salt
4–6	tsp (20–30 mL) extra virgin olive oil
1	lb (500 g) dried, flavoured corkscrew or macaroni pasta
½	lb (250 g) Provolone cheese, shredded
½	cup (125 mL) grated Romano Salemo cheese (2 oz/50 g)
1	tsp (5 mL) unsalted butter, at room temperature
2	Tbsp (30 mL) fine, dry breadcrumbs

Cooking instructions continued on following page . . .

TONY'S SUGGESTIONS
- FULL-BODIED, OAK-AGED, DRY RED WINE
  Zinfandel, Primitivo, Rhône red, Shiraz
- BEER
  Brown ale

MAKE AHEAD
- *This dish can be prepared to the baking stage 2 days ahead, covered, and refrigerated. If refrigerated, bake, covered, for 30 minutes, then uncover and continue to bake until hot in the centre, about 30 more minutes.*

GURTH'S NOTES
- *Use any other hard, grating cheese, such as aged Gouda, Parmesan, or Montasio, instead of the Romano.*

Sicilian Pasta Timbale (continued)
Cooking Instructions

1   **PREHEAT** the oven to 425°F (220°C) and place oven rack in the centre position.

2   **FOR THE SAUCE,** heat 1 tsp (5 mL) of the oil in a large saucepan over medium heat. Add the garlic and cook, stirring, just until fragrant, about 1 minute.

3   **ADD** the tomato purée. Bring to a boil.

4   **REDUCE** the heat and simmer, uncovered, until the sauce is reduced to about 3 cups (750 mL), about 20 minutes.

5   **ADD** the basil, season with salt and pepper, and set aside.

6   **FOR THE PASTA TIMBALE,** cut the eggplants lengthwise into ¼-inch (6-mm) slices.

7   **SPRINKLE** with the salt. Let stand for 30 minutes, rinse well, and pat dry.

8   **DEPENDING ON HOW MANY** eggplant slices you have, coat 2 or 3 shallow baking pans with oil, using 2 tsp (10 mL) of oil per pan.

9   **TURN** the eggplant slices in the oil to coat both sides. Arrange in a single layer in the pans.

10 **BAKE** in the preheated oven until the eggplant is brown and soft, about 10 to 15 minutes.

11 **IN A LARGE SOUP POT,** heat 4 quarts (4 L) of water to a boil. Add 1 tsp (5 mL) of salt and stir in the pasta. Cook until al dente.

12 **DRAIN** the pasta and mix with the provolone cheese, 2 cups (500 mL) of the marinara sauce, and 6 Tbsp (90 mL) of the Romano cheese.

13 **PREHEAT** the oven to 350°F (180°C).

14 **BUTTER** the sides and bottom of a 9-inch (2.5-L) springform pan. Dust the pan with the breadcrumbs.

15 **ARRANGE** ⅓ of the eggplant slices so they cover the bottom of the pan, overlapping them.

16 **COVER** with ½ of the pasta mixture.

17 **LAYER** ½ of the remaining eggplant overtop, then evenly top with the remaining pasta mixture.

18 **COVER** evenly with the remaining eggplant. Press down gently to compact the layers and make the timbale level.

19 **SPRINKLE** with the remaining 2 Tbsp (30 mL) of Romano cheese.

20 **BAKE** uncovered in the preheated oven until hot in the centre, about 30 minutes.

Stuffed Peppers
with Orzo, Chickpeas & Hot Chili Chèvre

Using Hot Chili Chèvre, produced by Salt Spring Island Cheese Company, Salt Spring Island, BC.

I created this recipe when I catered a Christmas dinner for the Officers' Mess of the Royal Regiment of Canada. I was told several of the guests were vegetarians, and I wanted to offer them a tasty dish that would be as festive as the usual holiday fare. Several of the omnivore guests requested this main course once they saw it, but I'd only made the quantity that was pre-ordered.

TONY'S SUGGESTIONS
- WHITE WINE WITH A TOUCH OF SWEETNESS, BUT GOOD ACIDITY
  Vouvray, off-dry Riesling, California Sauvignon Blanc
- BEER
  Belgian Saison, Porter

MAKE AHEAD
- *Orzo/cheese mixture can be prepared a day ahead, covered, and refrigerated.*

GURTH'S NOTES
- *Use any soft goat or sheep cheese, plain or flavoured.*

1	cup (250 mL) cooked orzo pasta
1	green onion, finely sliced
²/₃	cup (150 mL) canned chickpeas, drained and rinsed
³/₄	cup (175 mL) crumbled Hot Chili Chèvre
4	red bell peppers, tops cut off, seeds and core removed

Cooking Instructions

1 **PREHEAT** the oven to 375°F (180°C) and place the oven rack in the centre position. Spray a roasting pan with cooking oil.

2 **COMBINE** the pasta, green onions, chickpeas, and cheese in a bowl, mixing thoroughly.

3 **SPOON** the mixture into the empty red peppers.

4 **PLACE** the stuffed peppers in the prepared pan.

5 **BAKE** in the preheated oven for 15 to 20 minutes, or until soft.

PREPARATION TIME 70 MINS
COOKING TIME 15 MINS
MAKES 8–10 SERVINGS

Roasted Garlic, Cheese & Vegetable Fondue

**Using Swiss cheese, produced by Agrilait in Saint-Guillaume, QC,
and Emmenthal, produced by Fromagerie L'Ancêtre in Bécancour, QC.**

*Cheese fondues create a casual dinner ambiance where conversation tends
to flow more easily. Suspense is in the air! Who will be the first to lose their
skewered bread or vegetable in the molten cheese and who will enjoy the crispy,
cheesy crust at the bottom of the fondue pot. Go to page 27 for instructions on
how to roast garlic.*

1	lb (500 g) Swiss cheese, grated
½	lb (250 g) Emmenthal cheese, grated
3	Tbsp (45 mL) all-purpose flour
1	tsp (5 mL) freshly grated nutmeg
½	tsp (2 mL) freshly ground white pepper
1	+ ¼ cups (310 mL) dry white wine
3	bulbs garlic, cloves roasted, peeled, and mashed
1	French loaf, cut into ½-inch (1-cm) cubes
1	cup (250 mL) cauliflower florets, cooked al dente
1	cup (250 mL) broccoli florets, cooked al dente
1	cup (250 mL) baby carrots, cooked al dente
1	cup (250 mL) baby potatoes, cooked until tender

Cooking instructions continued on following page . . .

TONY'S SUGGESTIONS
- **MEDIUM BODIED WHITE WINE**
  *Sauvignon Blanc from the Loire,
  New Zealand or Ontario; Alsace
  Riesling*
- **RED WINE**
  Beaujolais
- **BEER**
  Lager

MAKE AHEAD
- *All vegetables can be cooked
  a day ahead, covered, and
  refrigerated.*

GURTH'S NOTES
- *Use other similar cheese, such
  as Gruyère or Appenzeller, to
  create this version of a classic
  Swiss fondue.*

Roasted Garlic, Cheese, & Vegetable Fondue *(continued)*
Cooking Instructions

1 **IN A LARGE BOWL,** combine the 2 cheeses with the flour, nutmeg, and white pepper.

2 **PLACE** a large heavy saucepan over medium heat and add 1 cup (250 mL) of the wine. Simmer until it has reduced by half. Stir in the roasted garlic.

3 **ADD** the cheese mixture a handful at a time, whisking after each addition until the cheese has completely melted.

4 **STIR** in the remaining ¼ cup (60 mL) of wine to reach the runny and gooey consistency you wish.

5 **TRANSFER** to a fondue pot and keep warm.

6 **ARRANGE** the bread cubes and vegetables on a platter near the fondue pot, and supply long forks for dipping the bread and vegetables into the cheese sauce.

Roasted Potato & Garlic Salad with Shaved Fennel & Feta, *page 197*

SALADS & SIDE DISHES

Lentil Salad
with Warm Goat Cheese

Using Hard Chèvre with Peppercorns, produced by Ran-Cher Acres in Aylesford, NS.

Lentils are so easy to use. Unlike many other dried legumes, they don't require overnight soaking. When rinsing them in cold water, watch for small pebbles accidentally mixed in with them.

8	oz (200 g) round Hard Chevre with Peppercorns
1	+ ½ Tbsp (23 mL) extra virgin olive oil
3	cups (750 mL) water
1	tsp (5 mL) kosher salt
1	cup (250 mL) lentils, rinsed and drained
3	sprigs fresh thyme
1	Tbsp (15 mL) unsalted butter
1	small red onion, diced
½	cup (125 mL) diced celery
½	cup (125 mL) diced carrot
½	cup (125 mL) diced red bell pepper
¼	cup (60 mL) chopped chives
1	Tbsp (15 mL) capers, rinsed and drained
2	pitas, halved and cut into triangles
8	radicchio leaves

TONY'S SUGGESTIONS
- DRY WHITE WINE
  Sauvignon Blanc from the Loire, New Zealand or Ontario, Alsace Pinot Gris
- SPARKLING WINE
  Spanish cava
- BEER
  Belgian

GURTH'S NOTES
- *Try this recipe using different flavours of goat cheese.*

Cooking Instructions

1 **PREHEAT** the oven to 375°F (190°C) and place the oven rack in the centre position.

2 **CUT** the cheese round in half and slice each half into 4 semi-circles.

3 **PLACE** in an ovenproof dish and drizzle with the oil.

4 **BRING** a pot with the water and salt to a boil and add the rinsed lentils. Reduce the heat to a simmer, add the thyme, and cook until the lentils are just firm, approximately 15 to 20 minutes. Drain the lentils and set aside.

5 **IN A SMALL SKILLET,** melt the butter over medium heat. Add the onion, celery, carrot, and red pepper. Cook until just tender, about 5 to 7 minutes.

6 **REMOVE** the skillet from the heat; add the chives and capers.

7 **PLACE** the pita triangles on a baking sheet and toast them in the preheated oven until crispy, approximately 3 to 5 minutes. Remove from the oven.

8 **PLACE** the goat cheese in the oven for 6 to 8 minutes, or until soft.

9 **MIX** the cooked lentils with the vegetables. Drizzle with more olive oil.

10 **FORM** 2 radicchio leaves into a cup, 1 cup per plate. Spoon the lentil mixture into the radicchio cups and place the warm goat cheese on top.

11 **GARNISH** each serving with the pita triangles.

Roasted Vegetables with Ricotta Pie

**Using fresh Ricotta, produced by International Cheese Co. Ltd. in Toronto, ON;
and Montasio, produced by Paron Cheese Company Ltd. in Hannon, ON.**

*Roasting is such an easy way of cooking vegetables, and this ricotta pie is a
perfect accompaniment. At the small store at International Cheese, I can buy
still-warm ricotta, made fresh that day. I often buy other types of cheese while
I'm there, along with other Italian ingredients.*

2	lb (1 kg) ricotta cheese
⅓	cup (75 mL) grated Montasio cheese
9	sprigs fresh thyme, leaves chopped
2	Tbsp (30 mL) chopped fresh oregano
•	kosher salt and freshly ground black pepper, to taste
2	eggs, beaten
3	Tbsp (45 mL) canola oil
½	celery root, peeled, cut into ½-inch-thick (1-cm) slices, then cut into small triangles
1	parsnip, halved and chopped
½	onion, coarsely chopped
1	bulb garlic, cloves separated and peeled
1	red bell pepper, seeded and cut into triangles
4	stalks celery, peeled and cut into ½-inch (1-cm) pieces
20	grape tomatoes
•	sprigs fresh parsley, for garnish

Cooking instructions continued on following page . . .

TONY'S SUGGESTIONS
- FRUITY, YOUNG RED WINE
  *Beaujolais, Valpolicella,
  Ontario/BC Pinot Noir*
- DRY ROSÉ
  Tavel or Bandol
- OFF-DRY WHITE
  Riesling, Gewurztraminer
- BEER
  Dark lager

GURTH'S NOTES
- *Find out who makes fresh
  ricotta in your area. It's
  amazing when you can buy it
  still warm.*

Roasted Vegetables with Ricotta Pie *(continued)*
Cooking Instructions

1 **PLACE** the ricotta in a cheesecloth-lined colander. Put a plate on top of the cheese, so it's pressing down on the cheese, and put a weight on the plate (such as a heavy jar of tomato sauce). Place the colander over a bowl to catch the drips and place in the refrigerator overnight to drain.

2 **PREHEAT** the oven to 375°F (190°C) and place the oven rack in the top third of the oven.

3 **IN A BOWL,** combine the drained ricotta (discard the liquid), Montasio, thyme, oregano, salt, pepper, and eggs. Mix well.

4 **SPRAY** a pie plate with cooking oil.

5 **SPOON** the ricotta mixture into the pie plate. Use a spatula to lightly press it down into the shape of the pie plate.

6 **BAKE** for 55 minutes, or until the top is golden.

7 **MEANWHILE, COMBINE THE OIL,** celery root, parsnip, onion, garlic, red pepper, and celery in a bowl. Toss well to coat all the vegetables with the oil.

8 **PLACE** the vegetables in a roasting pan and roast for 25 to 30 minutes, or until lightly caramelized. (The vegetables can roast during the last 30 minutes of baking the ricotta pie.)

9 **ADD** the tomatoes to the roasting vegetables for the last 5 minutes of cooking.

10 **FLIP** the warm ricotta pie onto a serving platter and surround with the roasted vegetables. Garnish with sprigs of parsley.

Roasted Potato & Garlic Salad
with Shaved Fennel & Feta *(pictured on page 190)*

Using Feta, produced by Holmestead Cheese Sales in Aylesford, NS.

"Where's the garlic?" was Joanne's comment upon tasting the initial version of this recipe. A smart husband always listens to his wife's comments. A second bulb of garlic was added. We both believe in the health benefits of eating lots of garlic and tend to double or triple the quantity of garlic suggested when we follow someone else's recipe. This recipe is for the garlic lovers out there.

1	+ ½ lb (750 g) baby new potatoes, halved
2	bulbs garlic, cloves separated and peeled
1	Tbsp (15 mL) dried rosemary
3	Tbsp (45 mL) extra virgin olive oil
1	small fennel bulb
1	cup (250 mL) diced feta
•	kosher salt and freshly ground black pepper, to taste

TONY'S SUGGESTIONS
- **MEDIUM-BODIED, DRY WHITE WINE**
  unoaked Chardonnay, Sauvignon Blanc, retsina, Assyrtiko (Greece)
- **RED WINE**
  Chilled Beaujolais
- **ROSÉ WINE**
  Bandol
- **BEER**
  Wheat beer

MAKE AHEAD
- *Salad can be made 3 hours ahead, covered, and kept at room temperature.*

GURTH'S NOTES
- *Try using feta made with cow, goat, or sheep milk. Each has a distinctive flavour and texture.*

Cooking Instructions

1 **PREHEAT** oven to 350°F (180°C) and place the rack in the centre position.

2 **IN A MEDIUM BOWL,** combine the potatoes, garlic, rosemary, and 2 Tbsp (30 mL) of the oil. Mix well.

3 **PLACE** in a roasting pan and roast in the preheated oven for 20 to 25 minutes, or until the potatoes and garlic are golden.

4 **USING** a mandoline or a very sharp knife, shave or cut very thin slices of the fennel bulb.

5 **IN A LARGE BOWL,** mix the fennel slices and feta. Add the potatoes and garlic.

6 **ADD** the remaining 1 Tbsp (15 mL) of oil and toss to combine.

7 **SEASON** with salt and pepper.

8 **SERVE** hot or at room temperature.

Gratinée Nest of Baked Spaghetti Squash

Using Saint-Pierre de Saurel, produced by Laiterie Chalifoux Inc./Fromages Riviera in Sorel-Tracy, QC.

Spaghetti squash is a neglected vegetable. Few people eat it and many more do not know how to cook it. Gurth to the rescue! We had one sitting in the kitchen for a week. Time for me to get creative and use it! Joanne and I had guests coming over for dinner that night. Unbeknownst to them, they were to be inducted into my Guinea Pig Club of recipe tasters.

1	spaghetti squash, halved lengthwise
2	green onions, sliced
2	eggs, beaten
•	kosher salt and freshly ground black pepper, to taste
½	cup (125 mL) broccoli florets, steamed al dente
½	cup (125 mL) cauliflower florets, steamed al dente
3	oz (75 g) Saint-Pierre de Saurel cheese, rind removed, sliced

Cooking Instructions

1 **PREHEAT** the oven to 350°F (180°C) and place the oven rack in the centre position. Lightly oil a baking sheet and 4 individual gratin dishes.

2 **PLACE** the spaghetti squash, cut side down, on the prepared baking sheet and roast for 30 to 40 minutes, or until tender. Remove from the oven and let cool.

3 **USING A FORK,** scrape the long, spaghetti-like strands from the inside of the squash into a bowl.

4 **MIX** in the green onion and eggs. Season with salt and pepper.

5 **SPREAD** the mixture onto the bottom and up the sides of the individual gratin dishes.

6 **PLACE** the steamed broccoli and cauliflower in the centre of the squash nest. Season with salt and pepper.

7 **COVER** with the cheese slices.

8 **PLACE** the dishes on a baking sheet and place in the oven. Cook for 10 to 15 minutes, or until the cheese has melted and the vegetables are hot.

TONY'S SUGGESTIONS
- **DRY WHITE WINE**
  Sauvignon Blanc from the Loire, New Zealand, Ontario; Grüner Veltliner; Alsace Pinot Blanc; or off-dry Riesling, Gewurztraminer
- **FORTIFIED WINE**
  Palo Cortado sherry
- **BEER** *Dark lager*

MAKE AHEAD
- *Squash can be roasted and the broccoli and cauliflower steamed a day ahead, cooled, covered, and refrigerated. Bring to room temperature before assembling.*

GURTH'S NOTES
- *Use other melting cheese, such as Limburger, Edam, Esrom, Munster, havarti, or Oka.*

Tri-Cheesy Mashed Potatoes

Using Smoked Gouda, produced by Gort's Gouda Cheese Farm in Salmon Arm, BC; Old Sharpe, produced by Ivanhoe Cheese Inc. in Ivanhoe, ON; and Emmenthal, produced by Fromagerie L'Ancêtre Inc. in Bécancour, QC.

Give mashed potatoes extra flavour by adding grated cheese. Use whatever cheese you have in the fridge. Make it taste good!

2	lb (1 kg) Yukon Gold potatoes, peeled and cut into cubes
4	Tbsp (60 mL) unsalted butter, softened
½	red onion, diced
¾	cup (175 mL) milk
14	oz (350 g) mixed shredded cheeses (Smoked Gouda, Old Sharpe, and Emmenthal)
2	Tbsp (30 mL) chopped fresh sage
1	Tbsp (15 mL) dried mustard
6	sprigs fresh thyme, leaves chopped
•	kosher salt and freshly ground black pepper, to taste

Cooking Instructions

1 **PLACE** the potatoes in a large pot of cold water. Bring to a boil and cook until tender, approximately 15 to 20 minutes.

2 **STRAIN** the potatoes, place them back in the warm pot, and stir to let excess moisture evaporate.

3 **USING A POTATO RICER** or a masher, rice or mash the potatoes in a large bowl until smooth.

4 **IN A SMALL SKILLET** over medium heat, melt 1 Tbsp (15 mL) of the butter. Add the onion and cook until soft, approximately 3 to 5 minutes.

5 **ADD** the remaining 3 Tbsp (45 mL) butter and the milk. Heat until the milk is warm.

6 **TRANSFER** the mashed potatoes back into the pot. Stir in the onion/milk mixture, cheese, sage, mustard, and thyme. Mix well.

7 **SEASON** with salt and pepper.

TONY'S SUGGESTIONS
- MEDIUM-BODIED, DRY WHITE WINE
  Unoaked Chardonnay, Riesling, Spätlese, dry Orvieto
- BEER
  Bock, dark lager

MAKE AHEAD
- *Mashed potatoes can be made a day ahead, covered, and refrigerated. Reheat on the stovetop, and add more warm milk and butter.*

GURTH'S NOTES
- *Try making this dish with sweet potatoes. They won't take as long to cook and are more nutritious.*
- *Use your favourite cheddar, Edam, Esrom, or even a goat cheese.*
- *For a seasonal take, use a soft chèvre in spring, a washed rind cheese in summer, a nippy cheddar in fall, and a blue in winter.*

PREPARATION TIME 20 MINS
COOKING TIME 16 MINS
MAKES 4 SERVINGS

Frère Jacques & Lupini Bean Salad

Using Frère Jacques Cheese, produced by Abbaye de Saint-Benoît-du-Lac in Saint-Benoît-du-Lac, QC.

It had been a long time since Joanne and I had eaten lupini beans when I saw them at a local Italian specialty food store. I thought they would be tasty in a recipe for the book, so we bought a large tub. Beans are good for us as a source of fibre and B vitamins. Lupinis are popular in Mediterranean countries and are commonly sold precooked in a brine solution in jars (like olives and pickles) and can be eaten by removing the seeds from the tough outer pod.

2	cups (500 mL) lupini beans, precooked
2	cups (500 mL) finely sliced romaine lettuce
2	stalks celery, peeled and chopped
1	small red onion, diced
⅓	cup (75 mL) chopped carrots
¼	cup (60 mL) extra virgin olive oil
1	Tbsp (15 mL) balsamic vinegar
2	Tbsp (30 mL) lemon juice
1	tsp (5 mL) sugar
•	kosher salt and freshly ground black pepper, to taste
3	oz (75 g) Frère Jacques cheese, diced

Cooking Instructions

1 **PEEL** the outer skin off the lupini beans.

2 **IN A BOWL,** combine the beans, romaine, celery, onion, and carrots.

3 **WHISK** the oil, vinegar, lemon juice, sugar, salt, and pepper together.

4 **DRIZZLE** the vinaigrette over the vegetables and toss lightly.

5 **DIVIDE** equally among 4 plates and garnish with the cheese.

TONY'S SUGGESTIONS
- **WHITE WINE**
  Sauvignon Blanc from the Loire or Ontario/BC, unoaked Chardonnay
- **BEER**
  Lager

MAKE AHEAD
- *The vinaigrette can be made 2 days ahead, covered, and refrigerated. Bring to room temperature (as oil will solidify).*

GURTH'S NOTES
- *Substitute other beans, such as romano, pinto, or navy beans.*
- *Try other Swiss-style cheeses, such as Alpinois, Le Moine, or Emmenthal.*

Pear, Valbert & Walnut Salad

Using Valbert, produced by Fromagerie Lehmann in Hébertville, QC.

When I spoke to Marie Lehmann about her family's Valbert cheese, she mentioned that she likes to eat it with pears in a salad. From her suggestion came this recipe idea.

2	stalks celery, peeled and diced
½	cup (125 mL) walnuts, toasted and chopped
2	cups (500 mL) torn romaine lettuce
1	Anjou pear, peeled and thinly sliced
2	Tbsp (30 mL) extra virgin olive oil
1	Tbsp (15 mL) red wine vinegar
½	tsp (2 mL) Dijon mustard
•	kosher salt and freshly ground black pepper, to taste
4	slices Valbert cheese

Cooking Instructions

1   **IN A LARGE BOWL,** combine the celery, walnuts, lettuce, and pear slices. Toss lightly.
2   **WHISK** the oil, vinegar, mustard, salt, and pepper together.
3   **DRIZZLE** the vinaigrette over the salad and toss gently.
4   **SERVE** on individual plates and garnish each with a slice of cheese.

TONY'S SUGGESTIONS
- **SWEETISH WHITE WINE WITH GOOD ACIDITY**
  Semi-dry Vouvray, Viognier, Riesling Spätlese, or Ontario Late Harvest Riesling
- **SPARKLING WINE**
  Asti Spumante
- **BEER**
  Lager

MAKE AHEAD
- *Vinaigrette can be made 2 days ahead, covered, and refrigerated. Return to room temperature and whisk prior to using.*

GURTH'S NOTES
- *Use a firm Swiss-style cheese, such as Emmenthal, Rathtrevor, Alpine Meadow, Honeywood, or Le Moine.*

Yukon Gold, Sweet Potato & Celeriac Cajun Gratin

Using Cajun Cheddar, produced by D Dutchmen Dairy Ltd. in Sicamous, BC.

At Christmas dinner with my paternal grandparents, my family celebrated by sharing the traditional English feast of roast turkey, cranberries, and flambéed plum pudding. My favourite part of the meal was the potato gratin, and I'd often ask for seconds. I don't believe sweet potatoes and celeriac were as popular or available 30 years ago as they are today, but here's a new twist on my old favourite.

1	+ ½ cups (375 mL) vegetable stock
1	Tbsp (15 mL) fresh thyme
½	red onion, sliced
1	clove garlic, peeled
3	large Yukon Gold potatoes, peeled and thinly sliced
•	kosher salt and freshly ground black pepper, to taste
1	sweet potato, peeled and thinly sliced
1	celeriac, peeled and thinly sliced
1	cup (250 mL) shredded Cajun Cheddar
¼	cup (60 mL) dried breadcrumbs

TONY'S SUGGESTIONS

- **MEDIUM-BODIED RED WINE**
  Chilean Merlot, Oregon Pinot Noir, red Burgundy, Ontario or BC Meritage
- **SPARKLING WINE**
  dry
- **FORTIFIED WINE**
  Tawny port
- **BEER**
  Real ale

MAKE AHEAD

- *Potatoes, sweet potatoes, and celeriac can be sliced 1 day ahead, covered in cold water, and refrigerated.*

GURTH'S NOTES

- *Be creative—try this dish with any one of your favourite cheeses.*

Cooking Instructions

1 **PREHEAT** the oven to 350°F (180°C) and place the oven rack in the centre position.

2 **IN A SMALL SAUCEPAN** over medium-low heat, combine the vegetable stock, fresh thyme, and red onions. Simmer for 5 minutes.

3 **COAT** an 11- x 7-inch (2-L) baking dish with cooking spray.

4 **RUB** garlic on the inside surface of the baking dish.

5 **PLACE** a layer of potatoes in the dish and sprinkle with salt and pepper. Add a layer of sweet potatoes, and more salt and pepper.

6 **ADD** another layer of potato, salt and pepper, and a layer of celeriac. Repeat until all the ingredients are used or you reach the top of the dish. The final layer should be potato.

7 **POUR** the stock mixture over the vegetables.

8 **SPREAD** the grated cheese overtop of the vegetables. Cover with a lid or foil and bake for 70 minutes.

9 **REMOVE** the cover. Sprinkle the breadcrumbs on top and cook for another 25 minutes.

Maple Tiramisu, *page 208*

DESSERTS

PREPARATION TIME 1 HR
  + 6 HRS REFRIGERATION
COOKING TIME 5–7 MINS
MAKES 12 SERVINGS

Maple Tiramisu

(pictured on page 206)

Using Mascarpone, produced by Silani Sweet Cheese Ltd. in Schomberg, ON.

Here is my Canadian version of this delicious Italian dessert. I created it as the birthday cake for my mother-in-law, Kathleen. She and the rest of the family gave it the thumbs up.

27	ladyfinger cookies
3	oz (90 mL) vanilla cognac, such as Navan
6	egg yolks
4	Tbsp (60 mL) maple sugar
3	egg whites
1	lb (500 g) Mascarpone, at room temperature
½	cup (125 mL) maple syrup
5	pieces of maple candy, crumbled

TONY'S SUGGESTIONS
- **SWEET WHITE WINE**
  Muscat Beaumes-de-Venise, Samos Muscat, Ontario Vidal Icewine, Sauternes
- **SPARKLING WINE**
  Asti spumante
- **FORTIFIED WINE**
  Cream sherry, LBV port
- **BEER**
  Lager
- **SPIRITS**
  Cognac, Drambuie

MAKE AHEAD
- *Tiramisu can be made 1 day ahead, covered, and refrigerated.*

GURTH'S NOTES
- *If available, try using a maple whisky or maple liqueur instead of the vanilla cognac.*

Cooking Instructions

1 CUT 12 of the ladyfingers in half and arrange most of them along the sides of an 11- x 7-inch (2-L) rectangular glass dish (such as a lasagna pan).

2 COVER the bottom of the dish with a layer of whole ladyfingers. Use the halved pieces to plug large spaces.

3 BRUSH the cookies with the cognac.

4 IN A LARGE BOWL, whisk the egg yolks and 2 Tbsp (30 mL) of the maple sugar.

5 PLACE the bowl over a pot of simmering water. With a wooden spoon, stir the egg mixture until it lightens in colour and begins to thicken, about 5 to 7 minutes. Remove the bowl from the heat and allow to cool.

6 IN A LARGE BOWL, whisk the egg whites until stiff peaks form. Set aside.

7 COMBINE the mascarpone and maple syrup in a food processor and process until smooth.

8 WORKING in small batches, gently mix the mascarpone mixture into the cooked egg yolk mixture.

9 GENTLY fold the egg whites into the mascarpone/egg yolk mixture.

10 SPOON ½ the mascarpone mixture over the ladyfingers. Sprinkle 1 Tbsp (15 mL) of the maple sugar on top.

11 ARRANGE a second layer of whole ladyfingers overtop. Use halved pieces to plug large spaces.

12 BRUSH the second layer of ladyfingers with cognac.

13 COVER with the remaining mascarpone mixture and sprinkle with the remaining 1 Tbsp (15 mL) maple sugar.

14 GARNISH the top of the tiramisu with the crumbled maple candy.

15 COVER and refrigerate for 6 hours or overnight.

Raspberry Red Dawn Tartlets

Using Red Dawn, produced by Hilary's Fine Cheeses in Cobble Hill, BC.

Hillary Abbott uses one of my favourite beverages, a local hard apple cider, to wash his Tomme-style cheese, giving it a hint of apple flavour. YUM! If you ever meet my wife Joanne, ask her how much I love cider. A cider-washed cheese dessert sounds pretty good to me (pun intended).

1	+ ⅓ cups (325 mL) milk
3	Tbsp (45 mL) sugar
3	egg yolks
3	Tbsp (45 mL) all-purpose flour
¼	tsp (1 mL) pure vanilla extract
½	cup (125 mL) diced Red Dawn cheese, rind removed
12	tartlet shells, baked following manufacturer's instructions
12	fresh raspberries, for garnish

TONY'S SUGGESTIONS
- SWEET RED DESSERT WINE
  Cabernet Franc Icewine, Banyuls, sweet raspberry wine
- FORTIFIED WINE
  10-year-old tawny port
- BEER
  Lager
- CIDER
  Sweet apple cider

MAKE AHEAD
- *Custard can be prepared 2 days ahead, its surface covered with plastic wrap, and refrigerated.*
- *Tartlets can be filled and garnished 2 hours prior to serving.*

GURTH'S NOTES
- *Try using other flavoured, semi-soft, washed rind cheese, such as Délice des Appalaches (ice cider), Belle Ann (black currant), Cru des érables (maple liqueur), or Rougette de Brigham (apple brandy).*

Cooking Instructions

1 **IN A MEDIUM SAUCEPAN,** heat the milk over medium-low temperature until slightly warm.

2 **IN A SMALL BOWL,** combine the sugar and eggs; mix well for 3 minutes, or until the mixture is light yellow in colour.

3 **STIR** in the flour.

4 **ADD** 2 Tbsp (30 mL) of the warm milk to the mixture and stir well to temper the eggs. Do not pour all the warm milk into the eggs or they will become scrambled eggs.

5 **ADD** the warmed egg mixture to the remaining milk in the saucepan, stirring well.

6 **COOK** for 10 minutes, whisking continuously, until the mixture becomes a thick sauce.

7 **REMOVE** the saucepan from the heat and mix in the vanilla and diced cheese. Stir until the cheese has melted.

8 **POUR** the cheese custard into a bowl and place plastic wrap directly on the surface of the custard. Let cool at room temperature for at least 30 minutes.

9 **SPOON** or pipe the cooled custard into the baked tartlet shells and garnish with many fresh raspberries. Serve immediately.

Apple, Maple & Sheep Cheese Tart
with Almond Crust

Using Greek-style Sheep Cheese, produced by Shepherd Gourmet Dairy in Tavistock, ON.

This recipe comes from the files of Stewart Cardiff, founder of Shepherd Gourmet Dairy. The recipe produces two tarts: enjoy one with your family and share the other one with your co-workers, fellow bridge players, neighbours . . . Food is power! You can bribe people with it. Joanne suggests making this in a rectangular pan and cutting it into bars. (She loves bars and squares.) Preparing it this way would be perfect for a large family get together, a bake sale, or a church bazaar.

2	cups (500 mL) slivered almonds, toasted until golden
¾	cup (175 mL) all-purpose flour, divided
½	cup (125 mL) brown sugar
½	cup (125 mL) melted unsalted butter
2	Tbsp (30 mL) butter, at room temperature
4	apples, peeled, cored, and chopped
1	lb (500 g) Greek-style Sheep Cheese
4	eggs, lightly beaten
1	cup (250 mL) maple syrup

TONY'S SUGGESTIONS
- **SWEET WHITE WINE**
  Ontario or BC Icewine, Sauternes, Riesling Auslese, Vin Santo
- **FORTIFIED WINE**
  Tawny port, cream sherry
- **SPIRITS**
  Calvados
- **CIDER**
  Quebec Iced Cider

MAKE AHEAD
- *Tart shells can be prepared and cooked 2 days ahead, covered, and stored at room temperature.*
- *Tart can be prepared a day ahead, covered, and refrigerated.*

GURTH'S NOTES
- *Use any fresh soft chèvre or cream cheese instead.*

Cooking Instructions

1 **PREHEAT** the oven to 350°F (180°C) and place the oven rack in the centre position.

2 **IN A FOOD PROCESSOR,** combine the almonds, ½ cup (125 mL) of the flour, and the brown sugar. Process until fine.

3 **ADD** the ½ cup (125 mL) of melted butter and pulse just to mix.

4 **PRESS** the dough into the bottom and up the sides of two 9-inch (23-cm) pie plates. Chill for 30 minutes.

5 **BAKE** in the oven for 15 minutes, or until golden. Cool thoroughly. Reduce the oven temperature to 325°F (160°C).

6 **MELT** the remaining 2 Tbsp (30 mL) butter in a skillet over medium heat, add the apples, and fry until golden and soft, about 10 minutes. Set aside to cool.

7 **IN A BOWL,** combine the cheese, eggs, maple syrup, and remaining ¼ cup (60 mL) of flour. Mix vigorously by hand until smooth. (A processor can be used as long as the mixture is not overworked.)

8 **ADD** the cooked apples to the cheese mixture and pour into the cooled tart shell.

9 **BAKE** for 35 to 40 minutes, or until the filling is golden and just set.

10 **COOL** and serve at room temperature.

Chambo-Chèvre Chocolate Cups

Using Fromage à la Crème, produced by Fromagerie Ruban Bleu in Saint-Isidore, QC.

On our way to the Warwick Cheese Festival last year, Joanne and I stopped to visit Fromagerie Ruban Bleu. They are located south of Châteauguay, on the south shore of the St. Lawrence River, near Montreal. As Mme. Claude de Margerie, the cheesemaker, was giving me a tour of all the cheese she produces, Joanne noticed small chocolate cups filled with cheese. Claude noticed Joanne's curiosity and offered her one. Joanne loves chocolate. What a match made in heaven, chocolate and cheese! We thought it would be tasty to add a touch more flavour to the cheese by adding a liqueur. This is a simple and delicious dessert that can be made and enjoyed by everyone.

½	cup (125 mL) Fromage à la Crème, plain
2	Tbsp (30 mL) sugar
5	tsp (25 mL) Chambord
10	small chocolate cups
10	fresh raspberries, for garnish

Cooking Instructions

1 **IN A SMALL BOWL**, combine the cheese, sugar, and liqueur, mixing until smooth and well combined.

2 **FILL** a small piping bag fitted with a small star tip half-full with the mixture. Pipe it into each chocolate cup.

3 **GARNISH** with a raspberry.

TONY'S SUGGESTIONS
- **SWEET RED WINE**
  Banyuls, Cabernet Franc Icewine
- **FORTIFIED WINE**
  Cream sherry, tawny port
- **LIQUEUR**
  Chambord, Bailey's

MAKE AHEAD
- *Cheese mixture can be prepared 2 days ahead, covered, and refrigerated.*
- *Chocolate cups can be filled with the cheese a day ahead, covered, and refrigerated.*

GURTH'S NOTES
- *Chambord is a black raspberry flavoured French liqueur. Use whatever you enjoy that you have in your liquor cabinet, such as Grand Marnier, Crème de menthe, Cassis, or Amaretto.*
- *You can use soft sheep cheese or cream cheese instead of the soft goat cheese in the recipe.*

Chevrotina & Pear Pastries

Using Ash Chevrotina, produced by Goat's Pride Dairy at McLennan Creek in Abbotsford, BC.

This recipe is derived from Cooking with Booze, *written by David Steel and Ryan Jennings. I was so impressed with the recipes and the food photography in their book that I bought two copies. These guys must have had a lot of fun testing their food and drink recipes. Joanne and I have used their book on several occasions, loving every recipe we prepared. I modified their Brie and Pear Pastries recipe by using Jason Dykstra's Ash Chevrotina cheese from Goat's Pride Dairy. I promised Ryan and David a favour/recipe/idea or my first-born, to be claimed at a later date. I hope it's not one of my recipes they'll be asking for—they are my babies!*

12	oz (300 g) Ash Chevrotina, rind removed, at room temperature
2	eggs
1	egg yolk
⅓	cup (75 mL) unsalted butter
¼	cup (60 mL) packed brown sugar
3	ripe but firm Anjou pears, peeled, cored, and sliced lengthwise
2	sheets puff pastry, thawed
1	Tbsp (15 mL) granulated sugar

TONY'S SUGGESTIONS
- **LATE HARVEST WHITE WINE**
  Riesling Auslese, Sauternes, Canadian Icewine
- **SPIRITS**
  Poire William

MAKE AHEAD
- *Cheese mixture and pears can be prepared and cooked 2 days ahead, covered, and refrigerated.*

GURTH'S NOTES
- *Use other similar soft, bloomy rind cheese such as brie, Camembert, Riopelle de L'Isle, Snow Road, or Le Noble.*

Cooking Instructions

1   **IN A FOOD PROCESSOR,** combine the cheese, 1 of the eggs, and the egg yolk. Process until smooth. Transfer the mixture to a bowl, cover, and refrigerate until required.

2   **IN A MEDIUM-SIZED SKILLET,** melt the butter over medium-high heat. Add the sugar and cook for 1 minute.

3   **ADD** the pear slices and cook for 1 to 2 minutes, or until the pears have softened slightly. Transfer the pears and syrup to a bowl, cover, and refrigerate until required.

4   **PREHEAT** the oven to 450°F (230°C) and set the oven rack in the middle position. Line a baking sheet with parchment paper.

5   **LIGHTLY** flour a work surface and roll 1 sheet of puff pastry into a rectangle large enough that 2 large squares can be cut from it. Repeat with the second sheet of dough.

6   **IN A MEASURING CUP,** beat the remaining egg with 1 Tbsp (15 mL) of water.

7   **SPREAD** equal amounts of the cheese mixture diagonally onto half of each pastry square, leaving a ½-inch (1-cm) border all around.

8   **TOP** the cheese mixture with the cooked pear slices.

9   **BRUSH** the edges of each pastry square with the egg/water mixture.

10 **FOLD** the dough over, forming a triangle. Seal the edges.

11 **MAKE** 3 slits on top of the pastry with a paring knife; lightly brush the top with more of the egg mixture, and sprinkle with the granulated sugar.

12 **PLACE** the filled pastry squares on the prepared baking sheet. Bake in the preheated oven for 5 minutes, then reduce the heat to 375°F (190°C) and continue baking for 10 to 15 minutes, or until the pastry is golden brown and the pears are cooked through.

13 **SERVE** warm.

Chocolate Mascarpone Purses
with Raspberry Coulis

Using Mascarpone, produced by Silani Sweet Cheese Ltd. in Schomberg, ON.

Working with phyllo dough is easy once you learn this basic trick: phyllo dough is thin and dries very quickly, so cover the unused sheets with a dry tea towel. Don't cover it with a damp tea towel, which will make the sheets soggy and impossible to separate one from the other. Once you've removed the phyllo you need for this recipe, roll the unused sheets together and wrap them very tightly with plastic wrap before freezing them again. I thaw a box of phyllo, use it and freeze the remaining sheets for future use up to three times before the sheets crack too much. It's great to be able to use one box of dough for several recipes on different occasions.

1	cup (250 mL) Mascarpone cheese, at room temperature
2	tsp (10 mL) pure unsweetened cocoa powder
2	Tbsp (30 mL) sugar
½	cup (125 mL) frozen raspberries, thawed
•	honey, to taste
4	phyllo sheets, thawed, at room temperature
½	cup (125 mL) unsalted butter, melted
•	fresh mint leaves, for garnish
•	fresh raspberries, for garnish

TONY'S SUGGESTIONS
- **SWEET WHITE WINE**
  Late Harvest Vidal, Cabernet Franc Icewine
- **SWEET RED WINE**
  Banyuls
- **FORTIFIED WINE**
  Tawny port
- **BEER**
  Fruit beer
- **LIQUER**
  Cream liqueur

MAKE AHEAD
- *Raspberry coulis can be made 2 days ahead, covered, and refrigerated.*

Cooking Instructions

1 **PREHEAT** the oven to 425°F (220°C) and place the oven rack in the centre position. Line a baking sheet with parchment paper.

2 **IN A SMALL BOWL,** mix the cheese with the cocoa. Stir in the sugar and set aside.

3 **TO MAKE THE RASPBERRY COULIS,** purée the raspberries in a blender. Strain through a fine mesh into a bowl to remove the seeds. Sweeten to taste with the honey and set aside.

4 **PLACE** a sheet of phyllo dough on a clean work surface. Cover the remaining sheets with a dry tea towel.

5 **LIGHTLY** brush the melted butter onto the sheet. Cut the phyllo dough into 4 equal-sized rectangles.

6 **PLACE** a rectangle on the work surface.

7 **COVER** with a second rectangle, turned at a 45° angle. Repeat with the third and fourth pieces.

8 **SPOON** ¼ of the cocoa/mascarpone mixture into the centre of the stacked phyllo.

9 **BRING** the edges of the phyllo together and press together to seal. Lightly brush the outer edges of the phyllo purse with the melted butter.

10 **PLACE** the completed purse on the prepared baking sheet. Repeat with the remaining sheets of phyllo dough.

11 **PLACE** in the preheated oven and bake for 10 to 15 minutes, or until the phyllo is golden brown.

12 **REMOVE** from the oven and let cool briefly.

13 **PLACE** a purse on each plate; drizzle raspberry coulis along the edge of the plate and garnish with a sprig of mint and fresh raspberries.

Port Cheddar Apple Tarte Tatin

Using Port Cheddar, produced by Fromagerie Perron in Saint-Prime, QC.

One day when I was visiting a cookware store, I saw a copper tarte Tatin dish. It was beautiful—and expensive! I have a love for copper cookware, but not for its price. It was at this moment that I came up with the idea of incorporating port cheddar into this classic French upside-down apple pie recipe. This dessert is named after the Tatin sisters, who created the recipe at their hotel in the late 19th century.

2	+ ¾ cups (675 mL) pastry flour
1	+ ¼ cups (310 mL) unsalted butter, at room temperature
1	tsp (5 mL) kosher salt
½	cup (125 mL) water (approximately)
½	cup + 2 Tbsp (155 mL) sugar
5–6	apples, peeled, quartered, and cored
7	oz (175 g) Port Cheddar, crumbled

Cooking instructions continued on following page . . .

TONY'S SUGGESTIONS
- **SWEET WHITE WINE**
  Icewine, Sauternes
- **FORTIFIED WINE**
  Cream sherry, tawny port
- **SPIRITS**
  Calvados
- **CIDER**
  Quebec Ice Cider, sweet cider

MAKE AHEAD
- *Dough can be prepared a day ahead, wrapped in plastic, and refrigerated. Let sit at room temperature for 30 minutes before rolling.*
- *Cooked tart can be made 2 days ahead, covered, and stored at room temperature.*

GURTH'S NOTES
- *Try using firm pears and your favourite cheddar or a cider-washed cheese, such as Red Dawn or Délices des Appalaches.*
- *Empire apples work well for this recipe!*

Port Cheddar Apple Tarte Tatin *(continued)*
Cooking Instructions

1. **IN A BOWL,** sift the flour and combine it with ½ cup (125 mL) of the softened butter, using your fingers to combine it with the flour so it resembles small grains.

2. **MAKE** a well in the centre of the mixture and add the salt. Pour in the water.

3. **STIR** the mixture to form a dough. You may need up to ¼ cup (60 mL) more water if it is too dry, but it should not be a soft dough.

4. **GENTLY KNEAD** the dough 12 times, until smooth; form into a ball. Enclose in plastic wrap and refrigerate for 30 minutes.

5. **PREHEAT** the oven to 350°F (180°C) and place the oven rack in the centre position.

6. **IN** a large ovenproof skillet, melt the remaining ¾ cup (175 mL) of butter over medium heat.

7. **EVENLY DISTRIBUTE** the sugar over the butter and, without stirring, place the quartered apples flat side down next to one another in a circular pattern, starting from the outside in.

8. **CONTINUE** to cook over medium heat until the sugar begins to caramelize and turns a light golden colour, about 10 minutes.

9. **PLACE** the skillet in the hot oven and bake for 10 to 15 minutes.

10. **REMOVE** the pan from the oven and sprinkle the crumbled cheese over the apples.

11. **ON A LIGHTLY FLOURED WORK SURFACE,** roll the dough so it forms a circle large enough to overlap the edges of the skillet. Place the dough over the cheese and tuck it inside the skillet. Return the skillet to the oven and bake for 15 minutes.

12. **REMOVE** from the oven and let cool for 5 minutes.

13. **PLACE** a serving plate upside down over the pan and carefully flip the pie onto the plate. Serve warm.

Quark-Filled Croquembouche

Using Plain Quark, produced by Fox Hill Cheese House in Port Williams, NS.

A croquembouche is a conical tower of filled profitéroles (cream puffs), bound together with caramel. It is tradition to serve this elaborate and delicious pastry creation at wedding receptions in France. It makes a beautiful table centrepiece. Why not fill them with a cocoa-flavoured quark cheese instead of pastry cream? Don't knock it until you try it.

FOR THE PROFITÉROLES

2	cups (500 mL) water
1	cup (250 mL) unsalted butter
1	tsp (5 mL) kosher salt
1	Tbsp (15 mL) sugar
2	cups (500 mL) all-purpose flour
6	eggs

FOR THE FILLING

1	cup (250 mL) Plain Quark cheese
2	Tbsp (30 mL) unsweetened cocoa powder
5	Tbsp (75 mL) sugar

FOR THE CARAMEL

1	+ ½ cups (375 mL) sugar

Cooking instructions continued on following page . . .

TONY'S SUGGESTIONS
- **SWEET WHITE WINE**
  Ontario or BC Icewine, sweet Malvasia, Commandaria (Cyprus Muscat), Rivesaltes
- **RED WINE**
  Banyuls
- **FORTIFIED WINE**
  Late bottled vintage port, cream sherry, Malmsey (Madeira)
- **SPARKLING WINE**
  Champagne Doux, Asti Spumante
- **BEER**
  Dark lager
- **LIQUERS**
  Southern Comfort, cream liqueurs, chocolate grappa

MAKE AHEAD
- *Pastry balls can be baked a week ahead, covered, and frozen. Thaw at room temperature prior to filling them.*
- *The cheese/cocoa mixture can be made 1 day ahead, covered, and refrigerated. Warm to room temperature before using.*

GURTH'S NOTES
- *Try using cream cheese, soft, fresh chèvre, or sheep cheese, and flavour it to your liking.*

Quark-Filled Croquembouche (continued)
Cooking Instructions

1 **PREHEAT** the oven to 425°F (220°C) and place the oven rack in the centre position.

2 **FOR THE PROFITEROLES,** combine the water, butter, salt, and 1 Tbsp (15 mL) sugar in a saucepan. Bring to a boil. Remove the pan from the heat and stir in the flour.

3 **RETURN** the pan to medium-low heat and cook, stirring, for 1 minute.

4 **REMOVE** the pan from the heat and add the eggs 1 at a time, stirring until each egg is well incorporated before adding the next.

5 **INSERT** a plain piping tip (# 5) into a pastry bag. Fill the bag half-full with the dough. Apply a small dab of dough to each corner of a large baking sheet. Cover the baking sheet with parchment paper and press it onto the dough, which will anchor it.

6 **PIPE THE DOUGH** onto the parchment paper, making each one approximately the size of a golf ball and spacing them ½ inch (1 cm) apart. You should have approximately 50 balls.

7 **BAKE** in the preheated oven for 10 minutes. Reduce the heat to 375°F (190°C) and bake for another 15 minutes. Remove and let cool.

8 **FOR THE FILLING,** stir the quark, cocoa, and 5 Tbsp (75 mL) sugar together in a small bowl. Taste for sweetness.

9 **INSERT** a small pastry tip (# 2) into a pastry bag and fill it half-full of the quark mixture.

10 **POKE** a small hole in each cooled pastry ball and pipe the quark mixture into it.

11 **FOR THE CARAMEL,** melt 1 ½ cup (375 mL) of sugar over medium heat. When the sugar begins to caramelize at the centre, gently stir the rest of the sugar into the centre with a metal spoon. Keep stirring until the sugar melts and turns a light golden colour.

12 **CAREFULLY PLACE** the hot saucepan in a larger bowl of cool water.

13 **WORKING CAREFULLY,** for the caramel is hot, dip 1 side of a filled pastry ball into the caramel and place on a large serving plate. Continue to dip the pastries, arranging them on the plate to form a ring of about 10 to 12 balls. This is the base of the tower.

14 **FOR YOUR SECOND LAYER,** dip the bottom and the side of the pastry ball in the caramel. Place on top of the first ring, angled slightly toward the middle. Continue dipping the pastry balls and forming layers until you have a decadent, cone-shaped tower.

Riopelle de l'Isle-Topped Maple Roasted Pears
with Orange Zest

Using Riopelle de l'Isle, produced by la Société Coopérative Agricole de L'Ile-aux-Grues on l'Ile-aux-Grues, QC.

I'm a huge fan of maple syrup and this is a favourite combination. Try this recipe as a variation on the classic poached pears.

⅓	cup (75 mL) maple syrup
3	Tbsp (45 mL) maple sugar
1	+ ½ Tbsp (23 mL) unsalted butter
1	tsp (5 mL) pure vanilla extract or paste
¼	tsp (1 mL) ground cinnamon
•	pinch freshly grated nutmeg
3	ripe Bosc pears, peeled, sliced in half lengthwise and cored
6	thin slices of Riopelle de l'Isle cheese
2	Tbsp (30 mL) orange zest

TONY'S SUGGESTIONS
- **FULL-BODIED, SWEET DESSERT WINE**
  Vidal Icewine, Sauternes, or Barsac
- **FORTIFIED WINE**
  Cream sherry, tawny port
- **BEER**
  Lager
- **SPIRITS**
  Southern Comfort, pear liqueur

MAKE AHEAD
- *The pears can be roasted and the syrup prepared several hours prior to serving; refrigerate. Reheat in the oven and broil with cheese just prior to serving.*

GURTH'S NOTES
- *Use a Canadian double or triple cream brie instead of the Riopelle de l'Isle.*
- *If maple sugar is not available, used packed brown or Demerara sugar instead.*

Cooking Instructions

1 **PREHEAT** the oven to 400°F (200°C) and place the oven rack in the centre position.

2 **IN A SMALL SAUCEPAN** over medium heat, combine the syrup, sugar, butter, vanilla, cinnamon, and nutmeg. Stir until the sugar has dissolved; set aside. Cut a slice off the rounded bottom of each pear half to make it sit flat.

3 **PLACE** the pears in a 12- x 13-inch (3-L) baking dish. Coat them on all sides with the syrup mixture.

4 **BAKE** for 20 minutes, or until the pears are just tender. Turn the pears over and baste with the syrup.

5 **TRANSFER** the pears, cut side up, onto a baking sheet. Place a slice of cheese on each pear.

6 **DILUTE** the syrup in the baking dish with a little water.

7 **INCREASE** the oven setting to broil. Broil the pears until the cheese begins to bubble. Remove from the oven.

8 **PLACE** a pear half on each plate and drizzle the syrup overtop.

9 **GARNISH** with the orange zest.

Cranberry-Orange Ricotta Torte

Using Ricotta, produced by International Cheese Co. Ltd. in Toronto, ON.

Most people think of using ricotta only in preparing lasagna and cannelloni dishes. Here's a recipe that shows how versatile an ingredient it is. Joanne measured and taste-tested the quantity of Triple Sec. She says it is just right. One detects a hint of the orange liqueur while savouring the torte's flavours.

2	cups (500 mL) Ricotta cheese
¼	cup (60 mL) 35% cream
1	cup (250 mL) sugar
2	Tbsp (30 mL) Triple Sec
1	Tbsp (15 mL) finely chopped orange zest
4	eggs
1	store-bought 9-inch (23-cm) chocolate crumb pie shell
¼	cup (60 mL) dried cranberries, soaked in warm water
1	orange, peeled and cut into segments

TONY'S SUGGESTIONS

- **SWEET WHITE WINE**
  Late Harvest Riesling, Icewine, Orange Muscat
- **SWEET RED WINE**
  Banyuls
- **FORTIFIED WINE**
  Tawny port
- **BEER**
  Fruit beer
- **LIQUEUR**
  Triple Sec, Cointreau

MAKE AHEAD

- *Torte can be made a day ahead, covered, and refrigerated. Garnish prior to serving.*

GURTH'S NOTES

- *Use organic oranges for the zest and segments. Chemical sprays on conventionally grown citrus fruit accumulate on the fruit's skin.*

Cooking Instructions

1 **PREHEAT** the oven to 400°F (200°C) and place the oven rack in the centre position.

2 **IN A LARGE MIXING BOWL,** combine the cheese, cream, sugar, Triple Sec, and orange zest and mix thoroughly.

3 **BEAT** the eggs into the mixture 1 at time, making sure each is incorporated before adding the next.

4 **POUR** the mixture into the pie shell.

5 **STRAIN** the soaked cranberries and carefully arrange them on top of the filling.

6 **PLACE** the pie shell on a baking sheet and bake for 10 minutes.

7 **REDUCE** the oven temperature to 300°F (150°C) and continue baking for 20 to 25 minutes.

8 **REMOVE** from the oven and let cool. Refrigerate for at least 2 hours before serving.

9 **WITH A KNIFE,** remove the membrane from the orange segments and garnish the torte with the segments.

Hazelnut Wafer Chocolate & Peach Mascarpone Gâteau

Using Mascarpone, produced by Silani Sweet Cheese Ltd. in Schomberg, ON.

One of my favourite cookies when I was a child was flavoured wafers. When my parents and I visited my paternal grandparents, I would raid their cookie box, hoping they had bought some. This recipe was inspired by a recent visit to a Polish fine food shop in Toronto`s Roncesvalle Village. Our good friends Donna and Andy like to shop there on occasion, stocking up on Polish delicacies. I saw the wafers and began brainstorming recipes in my head. Different flavoured wafers are available as well as plain ones.

9	oz (225 mL) Mascarpone
3	Tbsp (45 mL) peach jam
1	Tbsp (15 mL) unsweetened cocoa powder
3	Tbsp (45 mL) sugar
4	rectangular hazelnut-flavoured wafers (4 x 2¼ inches / 10 × 6 cm each)
12	toasted almond slices

Cooking instructions continued on following page . . .

TONY'S SUGGESTIONS
- **SWEET WHITE WINE**
  Late Harvest Riesling or Icewine or Quebec Iced Apple
- **SWEET RED WINE**
  Banyuls
- **SPARKLING WINE**
  Asti Spumante
- **FORTIFIED WINE**
  Ruby port
- **LIQUEUR**
  Amaretto, Frangelico

MAKE AHEAD
- *Gâteau can be made 2 days ahead, covered, and refrigerated.*

GURTH'S NOTES
- *Use your favourite jams and jellies, such as strawberry, raspberry, blueberry, or blackberry, to flavour the mascarpone.*

Hazelnut Wafer Chocolate & Peach Mascarpone Gâteau (continued)
Cooking Instructions

1 **IN A BOWL,** combine ⅓ of the mascarpone with the peach jam.

2 **IN A SECOND BOWL,** mix the remaining mascarpone with the cocoa and sugar.

3 **PLACE** 1 wafer on a plate, and spread with ½ of the peach-mascarpone mixture. Place a second wafer on top.

4 **COVER** the second wafer with a thin layer of the cocoa-mascarpone mixture. Place the third wafer on top.

5 **SPREAD** the remaining peach-mascarpone mixture on the third wafer. Cover with the last wafer.

6 **SPREAD** the remaining cocoa-mascarpone on the top and sides of the gâteau like icing. Cover and refrigerate for at least 1 hour.

7 **GARNISH** with the almond slices in a wheat stalk pattern. Smooth surface with a spatula if icing cracks.

8 **SLICE** the gâteau widthwise and serve.

Butter Tart Mascarpone Ice Cream

Using Mascarpone produced by Saputo Inc, in Saint-Léonard, QC.

If you haven't yet realized it, I am a huge promoter of Canada, and butter tarts are uniquely Canadian. I just love eating them with their centres still gooey and liquidy, and I've tasted several delicious versions during my travels across the country. Eganridge Inn in Fenelon Falls, Ontario, serves their large ones warmed up with a scoop of local Kawartha Dairy ice cream. Joanne and I visited a small bakery in Ganges, on Salt Spring Island, BC. As I bit into their syrupy butter tart, the idea came into my head to combine this sweet pastry with ice cream to make a frozen treat. YUM!

1	lb (500 g) Saputo Mascarpone
2	cups (500 mL) milk
1	cup (250 mL) sugar
4	store-bought pecan butter tarts, crumbled

Cooking Instructions

1 **IN A LARGE BOWL,** combine the cheese, milk, and sugar and beat with an electric mixer until smooth.

2 **FOLD** in the crumbled butter tarts.

3 **TRANSFER** to an ice cream machine and follow the manufacturer's instructions.

4 **TRANSFER** the ice cream to a container and place in the freezer.

5 **LET THE CONTAINER WARM** up at room temperature for 5 minutes prior to serving.

TONY'S SUGGESTIONS
- **SWEET WHITE WINE**
  Samos Muscat, Muscat Beaumes-de-Venise, Commandaria from Cyprus
- **LIQUEUR**
  Orange-based liqueur, Southern Comfort

MAKE AHEAD
- *Ice cream can be made 2 weeks ahead, covered, and frozen.*

GURTH'S NOTES
- *This is an easy way to make a rich ice cream without the hassle of making an egg custard sauce.*

Index

C